Angelica Hüseyinzade Şimşek
Prof. Dr. Mehmet Çakıcı

Erenköy Syndrome

Post-Traumatic Stress Disorder among Turkish Cypriot Soldiers of Erenköy Exclave Battle

Anchor Academic
Publishing

Hüseyinzade Şimşek, Angelica, Çakıcı, Mehmet: Erenköy Syndrome. Post-Traumatic Stress Disorder among Turkish Cypriot Soldiers of Erenköy Exclave Battle, Hamburg, Anchor Academic Publishing 2018

Buch-ISBN: 978-3-96067-215-9
PDF-eBook-ISBN: 978-3-96067-715-4
Druck/Herstellung: Anchor Academic Publishing, Hamburg, 2018

Bibliografische Information der Deutschen Nationalbibliothek:
Die Deutsche Nationalbibliothek verzeichnet diese Publikation in der Deutschen Nationalbibliografie; detaillierte bibliografische Daten sind im Internet über http://dnb.d-nb.de abrufbar.

Bibliographical Information of the German National Library:
The German National Library lists this publication in the German National Bibliography. Detailed bibliographic data can be found at: http://dnb.d-nb.de

© Anchor Academic Publishing, Imprint der Diplomica Verlag GmbH
Hermannstal 119k, 22119 Hamburg
http://www.diplomica-verlag.de, Hamburg 2018
Printed in Germany

ABSTRACT

The purpose of the present study is to determine combat related PTSD and severity occurrence rate among Erenköy Turkish Cypriot Fighters and Turkish Cypriot Fighters whom participated in the Cyprus War.

Importance of the present study is based on absence of any study related to Cyprus War participants, and Erenköy Turkish Cypriot Fighters.

The sample taken consist of 100 male Turkish Cypriot Fighters, 50 of them battled in Erenköy and 50 whom battled in other regions of Cyprus during Cyprus war in between 1963-1974. Structured interview for the present study was conducted, demographic information, pre-war, during war and post-war information was obtained.

Post-traumatic stress disorder (PTSD) was diagnosed using Clinician Administered PTSD Scale (CAPS).

As a result of the present study, it could be stated that Erenköy Turkish Cypriot Fighters are more likely to have a chronic PTSD, with Delayed onset, than Turkish Cypriot Fighters who served in other regions of Cyprus within period of war. Factors found to be trigger PTSD in scope of the present study are: lack of social support during the war and post war period, alcohol use, being adolescent during the war, presence of psychological disorders in pre-war period. Being not prepared mentally, less of military education, and military skills.

Key words: Post-Traumatic Stress Disorder, War, Post War Risk Factors to Post Traumatic Stress Disorder (PTSD)

1

LIST OF TABLES

ABBREVIATIONS

PTSD – Post Traumatic Stress Disorder

CAPS - Clinician-Administered PTSD Scale

1. INTRODUCTION

Posttraumatic stress disorder (PTSD) is a chronic and disabling psychiatric disorder which leads to exposure to a traumatic incident. PTSD is often diagnosed in between veteran population, as example among those from Vietnam War period. (Kulka et al. 1990), according to National Vietnam Veterans Readjustment Study, it has been determined that 15% of Vietnam veterans will meet criteria for PTSD diagnosis. Lifetime figures will be twice as much. And only for Australian Vietnam veterans figures will be 12% current and 21% lifetime, which is lower when compared to the rest. (O'Toole et al., 1996, 331-339). Such result of studies revel chronicity testament of disorder. Majority of Vietnam veterans with PTSD remain with such disorder currently as well (30 years after traumatic events). Eventually similar situation is applicable to Turkish Cypriot Fighters. The National Comorbidity Survey (Kessler, Sonnega, Bromet, Hughes, & Nelson, 1995, 1048-1060) has shown that over one third of persons with PTSD couldn't remit even after several years since trauma occurred.

Cyprus War differentiates from other wars, when considering effects of psychological traumas and related problems of veterans.

The Cyprus War – Erenköy Battle could be called first war fought by adolescents. World War II soldiers were 26 years old in average, while Erenköy Exclave fighters were 21 years old in average. Those individuals were in formative years, which made them extremely psychologically irrresistive to combat terrors imprints. Morals and values learned at home soon become stripped and the ego structure built through years became impaired. Experience of the battle caused by experience of a first kill or friend killed in the battle resulted psychological "snap" (B. Goderez, 1985). Teenage years and related development of the personality were stolen which caused abrupt halt of the maturing process. Currently majority of veterans are still struggling to complete maturing process, trying to "make it up for the lost time". Another issue is that parent role models were replaced by military officers.

Admonition to kill was highly contrasting with shalt not to kill. , which resulted in psychiatric disturbances. Discredit of the Cyprus War – Erenköy Battle led to an atmosphere of national confusion and antagonism. Campus demonstrations, draft card burnings, riots, and draft evaders represented the mood of the period.

Adverse feedback to the war was not restrained to Turkey. Turkish Cypriot fighters we were not welcomed enthusiastically, and therefore soon those young boys doubt what for they are risking their lives.

There were no battlefields or front lines defined which led to confusion whether territories are to be captured and held. Find and destroy became popular phrase among fighters, as during the war they searched for enemy who generally was unseen. Often enemy included children and women, also childhood friends, neighbors, teachers etc. under such circumstances it was hard to decide who the enemy is. Battle boundaries were extremely unclear. Surrounding nature and continuous heat worsen overall conditions. Experiencing and witnessing psychological conditions reigned moral confusion. (S. Huppenbauer, 1982, 1699-1703)

Fighters of Cyprus War had no chance of socialization while traveling to battlefields and back home in groups, no journey home for debriefing, processing the experience and assimilation into civilian life were more complicated for Cyprus War fighters.

Unit morale and support system necessary for soldiers in combat were missing. Absence of those resulted in post war barrage and anxiety instead of return trip filled with joy and anticipation.

If we could name single overriding factor of PTSD, no doubt home coming would be that one. There is no other example in this culture where country will turn its back to the soldiers who were laying their lives for.

As opposed to the World War II veterans who received cheers, welcomes and parades (Ozer, et.al. 2003, 52–73), the Erenköy fighters weren't even allowed to get back to their home country, instead they were forced to live abroad and deal with being alienated. There was little or no support by the Government. In the face of such difficulty, veterans were left on their own to retrieve what was left of their lives. They were not the same boys who used to fight for their country. They have done their duty, lost their friends, grow mature untimely, lost their own sense of self in the insanity of the war and were rejected at homeland, for which they had risked their lives.

Individual suffers from helplessness, depression, dejection, and severe grief with frequent thoughts of suicide. As seen in the study published in New England Journal of Medicine, men who served in Vietnam War were twice as much likely to commit suicide compared to those who didn't serve. That reveals that the number who died since returning home from war doesn't much differ from number of those who died at war 59.000 (Veteran, September, 1988). Among Erenköy Exclave Battle Fighters suicides occurred during the war and in post-war period.

Many veterans are enclosed in a death immersion; they haven't forgot, they dream it, and the dreams are ever present. It is common for them to own and carry guns even in daily life during post-war period. As it seen in Turkish Cypriot population. According to data from Northern Cyprus Hunting and Shooting Federation there are 22.000 active members.

Probably the most difficult is to separate PTSD and alcohol/substance abuse. Eventually, for many, it is inseparable. "It is not just substance abuse. It is not just PTSD. It's both of them wrapped up in one another," says Steve Bently, Chairman of the VVA PTSD and Substance Abuse Committee. "Alcohol and other drugs have successfully aided Vietnam veterans in covering their feelings for years. The biggest problem ... is that alcohol quits working after a while". "Trauma tries to surface, though the individual sufferings and to keep it submerged".

A study of Centers for Disease Control stated that Vietnam veterans were more likely to form depression, anxiety and alcoholism, around 500,000 experienced intense PTSD symptoms. (Brinson and Treanor, September 1988).

Individuals with PTSD symptoms are likely to develop alcohol and substance abuse as those are trying to find relief from the symptoms related to trauma experience. But such addiction may cause more serious problem and addiction shall be treated. (Brady, K.T. et. al.2004, 206-209).

1.1. Northern Cyprus

Northern Cyprus (or North Cyprus), officially Turkish Republic of Northern Cyprus (TRNC), is a self-declared state (Emerson et. al., 2004) that comprises northeastern portion of the Cyprus island. Recognized only by Turkey, Northern Cyprus is considered by international community as occupied territory of the Republic of Cyprus. (United Nations Security Council resolution 550 (1983)). Northern Cyprus extends from the tip of the Karpass Peninsula in the north east, westward to Morphou Bay and Cape Kormakitis (Kokkina/Erenköy exclave marks the westernmost extent of the area), and southward to the village of Louroujina/Akıncılar.

Since 1974, Cyprus is divided into a Turkish Cypriot north and a Greek Cypriot south, separated by a 180 km long UN-controlled buffer zone.

1.2. The Cyprus War

The 1974 coup d'état, an attempt to annex the island to Greece, was followed by Turkish invasion of Cyprus. This resulted in eviction of North's Greek Cypriot population majority, flight of Turkish Cypriots from the south, and partitioning of the island, leading to a unilateral declaration of independence by the North in 1983. (Leonard, 2006, 429).

1.3. Erenköy Exclave Battle

Erenköy is a village in Cyprus, administered by Turkish Republic of Northern Cyprus. It was one of the Turkish Cypriot enclaves prior to invasion of Cyprus in 1974. It is bordered on three sides by mountainous territory to the Greek part of the island, with the Mediterranean Sea (Morphou Bay) on its northern flank. The exclave sits several kilometers away from the mainland of TRNC and is a place, which has special symbolic significance for Cypriots, as per events of August 1964 (Sadrazam, 2013).

Since December 1963, thousands of Turkish Cypriots concentrated in enclaves, as a result of intercommunal fighting. Erenköy was one of the last port areas under Turkish Cypriot control and a vital supply link with Turkey for Turkish Cypriot Fighters (Menguc, 2005).

In this year's approximately 700 students was studying in Turkey in Universities. More than half of them were male. 500 of them with a help of Turkish Resistance Organization got unofficial military training at Ankara Zir village. Some of them got this training for 15 days, some for 3-4 days. After following those came to Cyprus (Erenköy) to battle. They have not any equipment: tents for shelter, appropriate clothes. They had very weak and old weapons. Those "Solders" should always remain watchful, to avoid being noticed by Cyprus Solders, and keep an eye on weapons and other aid coming from motherland (Vurana, 2011, 179-355).

In these days leading up to the invasion, the Cypriot National Guard began to mobilize infantry, artillery and armored forces for an assault on Erenköy. On 6 August 1964, the Cypriot National Guard commenced its attack (BBC 1964).

On 8 August 1964, after waiting for nearly two days, Turkey intervened, once it had become clear that Greek Cypriots would not withdraw from Erenköy, but simply commit more and more siege forces until Turkish Cypriots ran out of supplies (Sadrazam, 2013).

On the morning of 8 August, Cypriot patrol boats Phaethon and Arion were attacked by Turkish Air Force jets, as they sailed close to Xeros Harbor, Morphou Bay. (Menguc, 2005, 560-578).

On the 8–9 August 1964, Turkish Air Force was given free rein to attack multiple targets within the Dillirga coastal warzone, including a number of Greek Cypriot villages. Cypriot civilian casualties were reported as a result of heavy air attacks against several populated locations, including Lower Pirgo. Turkish planes also attacked sites occupied by the Cypriot National Guard, killing a number of military personnel. (Oberling, 1982).

In the eyes of the Greek Cypriot authorities, Erenköy was a threat to the nation's security posed by Turkish Cypriot paramilitaries, and cutting it off would have severed Turkish Cypriot armed groups from resupply and reinforcement.

During this battle Turkish Cypriot Fighters stay in enclave for 2 years. There was a lack of food, medical help because of weak intercommunication with executives. Within those 2 years they always were under pressure and blockade. Losses of Turkish Cypriot Fighters are: 12 martyr, 4 missing and 32 wounded.

When Turkish military staged their operation in Cyprus in 1974, Erenköy was a specific objective. The exclave became part of the Turkish Federative State of North Cyprus in 1975, followed by UDI in November 1983. However, this declaration of independence was condemned legally invalid by United Nations Security Council Resolution 541 (1983). (Henn, et. al., 2004, 240-360).

1.4. War

War is an organized and often prolonged conflict that is carried out by states or non-state actors. It is generally characterized by extreme violence, social disruption, and economic destruction. (American Heritage Dictionary), (Merriam Webster's Dictionary access date 25.01.2014).

War should be understood as an actual, intentional and widespread armed conflict between political communities, and therefore is defined as a form of political violence or intervention. The set of techniques used by a group to carry out war is known as warfare. An absence of war is usually called peace.

In 2003, Nobel Laureate Richard E. Smalley identified war as the sixth (of ten) biggest problem facing humanity for the next fifty years. (Smalley, et. al., 2008).

In 1832 in dissertation On War, Prussian military general and theoretician Carl von Clausewitz defined war as follows: "War is thus an act of force to compel our enemy to do our will." (Clausewitz et. al., 1984, 428-465).

While some scholars accept warfare as an inescapable and integral aspect of human nature, others argue that it is only inevitable under certain socio-cultural or ecological circumstances. Some scholars argue that practice of war is not linked to any single type of political organization or society. Rather, as discussed by John Keegan in his History of Warfare, war is a universal phenomenon whose form and scope is defined by the society that wages it. (Keegan, et. al., 1901).

Another argument suggests that since there are human societies where warfare does not exist, humans may not be naturally disposed for warfare, which emerges under particular circumstances. (Howell, et. al., 1989, 1-61).

1.5. Turkish Cypriot Fighters

Turkish Resistance Organization (TMT) armed organization was established in 1958, to fight against EOKA. Then in 1976 was renamed as Turkish Cypriot Security Forces. Its members called "mujaheed" – Turkish Cypriot Fighter.

1.6. Post-Traumatic Stress Disorder

The actual term Post Traumatic Stress Disorder – PTSD - enters the nosology in 1980. Kraepelin tried to make a categorization of psychological disorders, he suggested the term 'fright neurosis' (schreckneurose): defining anxiety symptoms after accidents and injuries. During World War-I diagnoses for reaction to combat were shell shock, combat fatigue and operational fatigue during World War-II and Korean War. After World War-II and during Korean War, DSM-I included 'gross stress reaction'. First DSM (American Psychiatric Association 1952) did not include list of detailed criteria, as now, but offered diagnosis for the people who were previously relatively normal, but experienced extreme stressors such as civilian catastrophe or combat, and had symptoms as a result of that stress. After in DSM-II (American Psychiatric Association 1968) this criterion was eliminated. This DSM-II was published during Vietnam War.

After, psychiatrists were unable to capture the symptoms of Vietnam solders. The official diagnosis of PTSD entered DSM-III (American Psychiatric Association 1980), after revision in 1980. (Friedman et. al., 2007).

Glass and Jones: PTSD symptoms can follow any serious psychological trauma, such as exposure to combat, accidents, torture, disasters, criminal assault and exposure to atrocities or to the sequelae of such extraordinary events. Prisoners of war exposed to harsh treatment are particularly prone to develop PTSD. In their acute presentation these symptoms, include subsets of a large variety of affective, cognitive, perceptional, emotional and behavioral responses which are relatively normal responses to gross psychological trauma. If persistent, however, they develop a life of their own and may be maintained by inadvertent reinforcement. (Glass, et. al., 2005).

The PTSD is an anxiety disorder that may develop following exposure to life-threatening or other inordinately distressing events. A diagnosis of PTSD requires that an individual experiences intense fear, helplessness, and horror in response to such an event, and that he or she experience pronounced symptoms of re-experiencing the traumatic event (e.g., nightmares or intrusive thoughts), avoidance of trauma-reminiscent cues and emotional numbing, and symptoms of increased arousal (e.g., exaggerated startle response or hyper vigilance).

Finally, these symptoms must be present for at least one month following the traumatic event, and must be of sufficient intensity to impair social, occupational, or other important domains of functioning. (American Psychiatric 1994.) Although most trauma victims experience pronounced emotional distress immediately following a traumatic event, the majority of these individuals will not go on to develop chronic forms of psychopathology such as PTSD, even if they do not receive formal, secondary prevention intervention. For instance, on average 8–9% of trauma victims develop chronic PTSD. (Kessler RC et.al. 1995, 1048-1060) (Breslau N, et.al.1998, 626–632).

For most of them, the adage "time heals all wounds" is an apt characterization of post-traumatic adjustment. However, large-scale events such as the terrorist attacks of 11 September 2001 can impact thousands of people. Accordingly, large numbers of individuals may go on to develop chronic distress following such an event, despite the fact that most victims can be expected to exhibit tremendous resiliency. In light of this fact, effective, early interventions for trauma are critical.

1.6.1. PTSD and Chronicity

PTSD recurrence differs in accordance with trauma nature. Morbidity changes at similar severity cases for the same trauma prove that PTSD trend is not quite linear (Goenjian A.K. et. al., 1994, 895-901).

DSM III (American Psychiatric Association 1980) characterized PTSD by positive prognosis, non-chronic and convinced that most of cases are treatable. However evidence collected during subsequent years explicit the opposite. Although lasting studies of natural disasters and hence examination of the long term affects revealed chronic nature of PTSD in 87% of cases (Patrick V, Patrick WK. 1981, 210-216).

Study related to the war trauma, soldiers receiving treatment within acute stage proceeded to chronic form in 50% of cases (Solomon Z, Banbenisity R., 1986, 613-617).

Enduring researches of general population divulge that PTSD symptoms are trending to continue over long years. Kessler and his friends in their study illustrate that one third of cases which meet PTSD symptom requirements even after ten years are likely to appear present. (Kessler R.C. et.al. 1995, 1048-1060). Furthermore, Davidson and friends in their study pointed out that 46% of developed PTSD had chronic nature (Davidson J.R.T., et.al.1991, 713-721), (Breslau N. et.al.1998, 626–632).

In a field study where 1007 individuals were scanned, 93% of the 394 persons who have filled questionnaires had PTSD. That research characterized disorder recurring after period of one year and over as chronic and 53 individual founded to have chronic PTSD. Such figures meet over 50% of the cases. Concurrently given group had highest number of PTSD positive cases when compared to other groups. "Overreacting" was determined in a high rate, as well as comorbidity (Breslau N, Davis GC. 1992 671-675).

Study on individuals imprisoned during World War II revealed that PTSD determined in a rate of 59% during first assessment, was still present in proportion of 29% even 40 years after (Speed, N. et.al., 1989, 147-153).

Research of Vietnam War veterans have shown that 31% PTSD symptoms rate at male individuals after 15 years turned to appear as 15% (Kulka RA, et.al. 1990a.).

Prisoners of war were heavily exposed to torture and several other traumas. In studies related to war PTSD rates determined were in a range of 30-88%. In studies made with American soldiers who fought in World War II high levels of PTSD were determined. PTSD ranges were 29-50%. Even though when many years passed sense recovery did not happen. (Solomon Z, et.al., 1991, 1-7).

The most important limitations during the studies occur because of different types and severity of traumas. The main long term picture of reactions appearing related to related are enounced as PTSD. At individuals who lived through war in Lebanon PTSD stopped as 63% rate measured one year after the war. After one more year that rate decreased to 43%. Even though there is decrease in figures as time passes by, that seems to be very slow process (Solomon Z, et.al., 1991, 1-7).

In the study of soldiers who served in southeastern Anatolia in Turkey, PTSD rates revealed as 5%, however in 95% of cases symptoms occur within one or two months since trauma all and are getting chronic. (Sungur M.Z. et.al., 1995, 279-284).

Opinion on gradually disappearing acute symptoms lasting through numerous years became invalid as time passed by. Umpteen times studies have proven such an illation. Common point of studies is based on idea that symptoms developed during acute stage will decrease over time, however such a process is very slow and vulnerable to secondary affecting. One of the most important evidences obtained in studies is that cases not meeting DSM IV (American Psychiatric Association 1994) diagnosis criteria exceed those diagnosed ones. At that point it can be said that there is parallel relation among the course of disorder and the course specified.

In the study made by Shore and friends (Shore JH, et.al.,1986, 76-83), study consist of three year observation after St. Helen's volcanic eruption, it has been determined that depression and anxiety symptoms are decreasing over the time, while PTSD symptoms were trending to have longer lifespan. A study made by Duggan and Gun revealed that one year after natural disaster PTSD rate is 39% and twenty six months after the event PTSD rate will fall to 23%. McFarlane (McFarlane AC, 1988, 30-39) indicated that 25 months after wildfire PTSD rates wouldn't change. However in studies of personal injury, rape, war and assault PTSD would be chronic in a majority (Breslau N, et.al. 1991, 216-222) (Foa EB, 1997, 25-28) (Resnick HS, et.al. 1993, 948-991), (North CS, et.al.. 1997, 1696-1702).Over 50% of cases were chronic (Ehlers A, et.al. 1998, 508-519).

However other traumatic events effect is more variable and is generally dependent of such factors as level of life danger, presence of physical injury, seeing injured people, loss of loved ones or witnessing injury of loved ones or their exposure to toxic substances (such as nuclear or chemical reagents) (Ursano R.J. et.al., 1995b, 36-42). At the same time those are factors determining severity of the trauma. Besides, secondary factors such as attempts to rescue depending on trauma nature, timing and efficiency, establishment of safe living areas and organization of health care services are being influential in those periods. Deficiencies during those periods consisting of physical, psychological and social support would reinforce negative effects of the trauma and may cause disease chronicity.

1.6.2. PTSD With Delayed Onset

If at least six months pass between the traumatic event and the onset of sufficient symptoms so that the full diagnostic criteria are met, the condition is diagnosed as "PTSD with delayed expression." Symptoms disappear within three months for half of adults, although some continue to experience symptoms over 50 years following the event (Solomon 1988, 323–329).

Concept of delayed post-traumatic stress was introduced in the early 1970's by a group of psychiatrists led by Robert Jay Lifton:

Delayed-onset PTSD describes a situation where a person does not develop a PTSD diagnosis until at least six months after a traumatic event. In some cases, the delayed onset of PTSD can be even longer. For example, some people may not begin to experience symptoms consistent with PTSD diagnosis until years after the experience of a traumatic event. Delayed-onset PTSD of this type has mostly been observed among the elderly, who may develop PTSD stemming from a traumatic event that occurred when they were much younger. (Andrews, B.et.al.2007, 748–766).

Studies have also looked at what factors might put fighters at greater risk for the development of PTSD with delayed onset. A number of risks among fighters have been identified. These include:

- Being previously in treatment for another disorder.

- Starting work as a firefighter at a younger age.

- Being unmarried
- Holding a supervisory rank in the fire service.

- Proximity to death during a traumatic event.

- Experiencing feelings of fear and horror during a traumatic event.

- Experiencing another stressful event (for example, loss of a loved one) after a traumatic event.

- Holding negative beliefs about oneself (for example, feeling as though you are inadequate or weak).

- Feeling as though you have little control over your life.

- Hostility. (Bryant, R.A., et.al., 1995, 267-271) (Zlotnic et.al. 2001, 404–406) (Gray et.al. 2004, 909–913).

PTSD ONSET

There are generally three different onset periods for PTSD. The types of onset are as follows:

a. Immediate Onset

b. Delayed Onset

c. Intermittent Onset

Immediate Onset PTSD

This type of PTSD onset occurs immediately or shortly after a traumatic event.

Some soldiers I have spoken with have experienced immediate onset PTSD after they watched one of their buddies get killed in Iraq. When the fire fight is over, or when they make it back to their hooch, they suddenly begin to have PTSD symptoms, such as a crying fit, going silent, or making a suicide attempt. The same can occur to survivors of sexual assaults. They immediately manifest PTSD symptoms such as sleeplessness, trust issues, and in some cases a suicide attempt.

Delayed Onset PTSD

Not every case of PTSD will manifest immediately after the traumatic event. It is not unusual for a period of time to go by before the symptoms surface. In many military cases we are seeing symptoms at 6, 9, and 12 months after returning from deployment. Many veterans who begin to show symptoms at the ten year mark after they left the service or after the traumatic exposure happened.

The first seven years of the Iraq war showed low reporting of PTSD for two reasons:

a. The perception, and sometimes the reality, that to admit to PTSD will damage your military career.

b. The military foolishly only asked about PTSD symptoms when soldiers and Marines were redeploying back to the States. Some soldiers reported that if you admitted to PTSD symptoms, then you had to stay two or three more weeks in Iraq while your buddies shipped home. That created a major incentive to not report symptoms. For a deployed service member, two to three more weeks in Iraq is an eternity.

The military was not doing follow up studies to see how often PTSD came up at the 6, 9, and 12 month intervals. These practices artificially lowered the reported rates of PTSD in returning service members. Delayed onset of PTSD can also surface in rape, war and clergy abuse survivors. PTSD does not have to begin immediately; sometimes it simmers for years before breaking out and ruining people's lives.

Intermittent PTSD

This is a variant of sorts of Delayed Onset PTSD. In a nutshell it means that at times the PTSD symptoms and behaviors will bubble up and manifest themselves and then after a time subside again. The periods of onset can be relatively brief, say a few hours, to a period of months. Intermittent PTSD is associated with PTSD triggers that activate memories, fears, anxieties, and physical reactions to trauma. The sound of gunshots or screaming might bring a person back to when they were shot at or raped. The smell of a person's cheap cologne may remind someone of being assaulted.

As one learns what their PTSD triggers are, they are able to be in better control and not be as vulnerable to PTSD. Various factors would affect incidents potential of being traumatic. Most important of those factors are age, genius and education level; nature and severity of trauma as well as meaning given to the incident by person; post-traumatic social, public and financial aid.

1.7. Post-Vietnam Syndrome

Vietnam War, (1954–75), a protracted conflict that pitted the communist government of North Vietnam and its allies in South Vietnam, known as the Viet Cong, against the government of South Vietnam and its principal ally, the United States. Called the "American War" in Vietnam. (Encyclopedia Britannica).

The figure of the traumatized veteran has become a commonly depicted character in the Vietnam War. PTSD as a clinical diagnosis has evolved in a large part from Vietnam Veterans. Disapproval of the war from American citizens was an important environmental factor accounting for veteran's post war stress. Prior to this time period veterans coming back from war were viewed as heroes, Vietnam War veterans came back home viewed as murders. Normally these war heroes were encouraged to talk about their war experiences but in this case they were not and were shunned by a lot of the community. More than 30 years after the end of the war in Vietnam, the effect of lingering stress on Americans who fought there continues to cause stress among researchers.

A new study finds that almost 19 percent of the more than three million U.S. troops who served in Vietnam returned with post-traumatic stress disorder (PTSD). It's a condition that left them with invasive memories, nightmares, loss of concentration, feelings of guilt, irritability and, in some cases, major depression. More than ten years after the war, 10 percent of them still could not leave the war behind. (Turner.F. 2001).

The term "Post Vietnam Syndrome" was developed by Dr. C.F. Shatan, past professor and Clinic Coordinator of the Post-Doctoral Psychotherapy Training Program of new York University. Dr. Shatan was working with New York members of VVAW (Vietnam Veterans against the War).

The syndrome consists of nine different aspects, some or all of which can be relative to individual.

1. Guilt feelings
2. Self-punishment
3. Feelings of being a scapegoat
4. Identification with the aggressor -- no outlet for bitterness and hatred
5. Dead place in oneself -- "psychic numbing"
6. Alienation -- xenophobia
7. Doubts about ability to love and trust other human beings again

8. Post-Vietnam Syndrome is really distorted mourning arising out of active discouragement of open grief by the military in a climate of death

9. Need to account for apparent absence of similar syndrome in W.W.II vets. Two are of particular interest -- unusual group cohesion and counter-insurgency training (with habituation to Universal Terror as chief weapon) (Shatan 1973, as quoted in Scott, 1990, 294-310).

2. METHOD

2.1. Participants

The present study was held from April 2014 until July 2014. Population of the study includes Turkish Cypriot Fighters and Erenköy Turkish Cypriot Fighters, which were recruited by phone call invitation. List with names and telephone numbers of Turkish Cypriot Fighters were obtained from the Turkish Resistance Organization, the numbers of Erenköy Turkish Cypriot Fighters were obtained from Erenköy Turkish Cypriot Fighters Organization. Then numbers were randomly determined. Participants were contacted by telephone and agreed to participate in the current study. The sample consisted of 100 male Turkish Cypriot Fighters, 50 of them battled in Erenköy (from total 562) and 50 comparison participants who battled in other regions of Cyprus during Cyprus war 1963-1974. All participants were given written informed consent. The structured interview for this study was conducted during 3 months period. Participants were interviewed on a voluntary basis by researcher of the present study.

Diagnosis of post-traumatic stress disorder (PTSD) was made with Clinician Administered PTSD Scale (CAPS) (Blake et al, 1995), a structured interview yielding PTSD diagnoses according to DSM-IV criteria (American Psychiatric Association, 1994). Participants first indicated their exposure to stressful life events on a standard life events checklist, a follow-up interview then assessed whether these events met criterion a (exposure to a traumatic event). The participant was then asked to choose the two most stressful of the events reported. The symptom interview focused on the presence of any PTSD symptoms related to the two events, over the participant's life as well as in the past month. Symptoms were assessed regardless of whether the selected events met criterion a, but the disorder was only diagnosed if both criterion A and the symptom criteria were met. Participants could receive up to two diagnoses of PTSD associated with the two events; however, cases of PTSD in the time intervals discussed above were calculated per individual. We asked whether events were related to the Cyprus war. In assessing the presence of war-era onset PTSD 40 years after the war, we assured that PTSD diagnoses were linked by event (if a person had war-era onset PTSD from event 1, we checked the duration of the PTSD related to event 1 to determine whether it was present 40 years later).

2.2 Instruments

Data for study was obtained by means of a survey questionnaires'. Demographic data collected using demographic information forms: separate form for Turkish Cypriot Fighters, separate form for Erenköy Turkish Cypriot Fighters and eventually CAPS scale form for both groups in order to set diagnosis of post-traumatic stress disorder.

2.2.1. Socio Demographic Information Form

Socio demographic information forms were prepared in two variations in order to highlight specific aspects of the Erenköy Turkish Cypriot Fighters. Both variants consist of three parts: pre-war, during war and post-war information.

Pre-war part of questionnaire includes information about: age, education, marital status, military education information, and presence of psychiatric disorders at pre-war period, participation in social groups and events related to pre-war political fluctuations. For Erenköy Turkish Cypriot Fighters questionnaire additional questions took place, those are: national plans, local plans, group number, period of stay in Erenköy.

Part of questionnaire about war period include following information: military rank, period of duty, presence of injuries, witnessing death or injury of another person, mental readiness, expectancy level, commitment level, slogged impact, social support.

Post-war part of questionnaire includes information: present level of education, present marital status, level of income, feeling of guilt, impact of the war, social support after war, medical support, alcohol consumption, illegal psychoactive drugs consumption, presence of psychological problems in close relatives, whether difficulties during war have been reflected to the society, support and amends received and expected from government and information about social appreciation.

2.2.2 CAPS-1

CAPS-1 a clinician-administered PTSD scale (Blake, et. al. 1995, 15-27). Turkish form reliability and validity study (Aker et. al., 1999, 286-293).

The CAPS is the gold standard in PTSD assessment. It is a 30-item structured interview that corresponds to the DSM-IV (American Psychiatric Association 1994) criteria for PTSD. CAPS can be used to make a current (past month) or lifetime diagnosis of PTSD or to assess symptoms over the past week. In addition to assessing 17 PTSD symptoms, questions target the impact of symptoms on social and occupational functioning, improvement in symptoms since a previous CAPS administration, overall response validity, overall PTSD severity, frequency and intensity of five associated symptoms (guilt over acts, survivor guilt, gaps in awareness, depersonalization, and derealisation).

For each item, standardized questions and probes are provided. As a part of the trauma assessment (Criterion A), the Life Events Checklist (LEC) is used to identify traumatic stressors experienced. CAPS items are asked in reference up to three traumatic stressors.

The CAPS was designed in order to be administered by clinicians and clinical researchers who have a working knowledge of PTSD, but can also be administered by appropriately trained paraprofessionals. Full interview takes around 45-60 minutes.

2.2.3 Statistical Procedures

Differences between Erenköy Turkish Cypriot Fighters and Turkish Cypriot Fighters on demographic variables were analyzed using IBM SPSS Statistics Ver.21 software. Some of demographic data as an average ± is given as a standard deviation. In the analysis data the number, percentage, chi-square, were used and a significance level of $p<0.05$ was taken.

Descriptive statistical methods chi-square, t-test and binary logistic regression were used.

3. RESULTS

Study was based on data collected from 100 participants. The mean age of participants was determined as 72.3±4,004 (60-90), p= 0, 40038. Mean age of each group separately is as following: Erenköy Turkish Cypriot Fighters mean age: 71.6±2.76 (67-83). While mean age of Turkish Cypriot Fighters: 72.9±4.9 (60-90).

Community membership rates among groups: Erenköy Turkish Cypriot Fighters %63.5 was members of Turkish Cypriot Culture Association, those organizing protests and other activities. Those members attended all events of communities' %92.0.

Turkish Cypriot Fighters %36.5 members of Turkish Resistance Organization. A quantity of evidence is %48.0.

Difference spotted between both groups revealed that Erenköy Turkish Cypriot Fighters were more bound to their objectives and willing to fight for their country.

Taken into account local plans of Erenköy Turkish Cypriot fighters when they were arriving to island: most of them wish to rescue their motherland %48, fight against Greek Cypriots %40, prevent events %4, fight and support %4, armament %4. And they have national plans like support their nation %44, rescue their family %36, if it is needed to become a martyr for their motherland %8, rescue their motherland %10, reunite with relative from South %2.

Erenköy Turkish Cypriot Fighters arrive on island in groups, namely in 10 groups. Arrival times differ from group to group, and accordingly period of their stay in Erenköy Enclave, hereinafter period of exposure to battle.%44 stayed on island for 22 months, %26 stayed for 20 months, %12 stayed for 18 months, %10, 21 months, %8 23 months.

Table 1. Comparison of Pre-War Education Levels among Erenköy Turkish Cypriot Fighters and Turkish Cypriot Fighters

Pre-War education levels	Erenköy Turkish Cypriot Fighters		Turkish Cypriot Fighters		Total	
	N	%	N	%	N	%
Non educated	0	0,0	17	34,0	17	17,0
Primary-High School	0	0,0	33	66,0	33	33,0
University Student	50	100,0	0	0,0	50	50,0
Total	50	100,0	50	100,0	50	100,0

χ^2= 96,222, df=2, p=0,000, not answered= 0

As Erenköy Turkish Cypriot Fighters were formed of University students, level of education of those was comparatively higher than Turkish Cypriot Fighters where one third were uneducated and majority were at Primary-High School level education. Pre-War education level of two groups was compared with Chi-square. A significant difference was found.

Table 2. Comparison Pre-War Marital Status among Erenköy Turkish Cypriot Fighters and Turkish Cypriot Fighters

Marital Status	Erenköy Turkish Cypriot Fighters		Turkish Cypriot Fighters		Total	
	N	%	N	%	N	%
Married	6	12,0	10	20,0	16	16,0
Single	35	70,0	38	76,0	73	73,0
Engaged	9	18,0	2	4,0	11	11,0
Total	50	100,0	50	100,0	100	100,0

$\chi2$= 5,578, df=2, p=0,061 not answered= 0

Majority of both groups members were singles. Marital status of groups was compared with Chi-square. No significant difference was found.

Table 3. Comparison of Military Education Rates among Erenköy Turkish Cypriot Fighters and Turkish Cypriot Fighters

	Erenköy Turkish Cypriot Fighters		Turkish Cypriot Fighters		Total	
	N	%	N	%	N	%
Educated	50	100,0	42	84,0	92	92,0
Non educated	0	0,0	8	16,0	8	8,0
Total	50	100,0	50	100,0	100	100,0

$\chi2$= 8,696, df=1, p=0,003 not answered=0

Military education of groups was compared by Chi-square, and significant differences were found.

Table 4. Comparison of Military Education Periods among Erenköy Turkish Cypriot Fighters and Turkish Cypriot Fighters

	Erenköy Turkish Cypriot Fighters		Turkish Cypriot Fighters		Total	
	N	%	N	%	N	%
No military education	6	12,00	8	16,00	14	14,00
1-10 weeks	44	88,00	15	30,00	59	59,00
10 and higher weeks	0	0,00	27	54,00	27	27,00
Total	50	100,00	50	100,00	100	100,00

$\chi 2= 41,230$, df=2, p=0,000 not answered=0

Military education periods for Erenköy Cypriot Fighters were not exceeding 10 weeks, while majority of Turkish Cypriot Fighters had much longer period of military education. Military education period before war among groups was compared with Chi-square. A significant difference was found.

Table 6. Comparison of Military Ranks among Erenköy Turkish Cypriot Fighters and Turkish Cypriot Fighters

	Erenköy Turkish Cypriot Fighters		Turkish Cypriot Fighters		Total	
	N	%	N	%	N	%
Enlisted	43	86,0	34	68,0	77	77,0
Commander	7	14,0	16	32,0	23	23,0
Total	50	100,0	50	100,0	100	100,0

$\chi 2= 4,574$, df=1, p=0,032 not answered= 0

In regards with military rank distribution among groups, it could be fairly said that higher military ranks are more common among Turkish Cypriot Fighters.

Military ranks range among groups was compared with Chi-square. Little difference was found.

Table 7. Comparison of Injury Rates during the War among Erenköy Turkish Cypriot Fighters and Turkish Cypriot Fighters

	Erenköy Turkish Cypriot Fighters		Turkish Cypriot Fighters		Total	
	N	%	N	%	N	%
Life threating injury	11	22,0	4	8,0	15	15,0
Injury which required outpatient treatment	12	24,0	7	14,0	19	19,0
No injury	27	54,0	39	78,0	66	66,0
Total	50	100,0	50	100,0	100	100,0

$\chi 2$= 6,764, df=2, p=0,034 not answered=0

Turkish Cypriot Fighter had higher rates of no injury as wellness life treating and other injuries. Injury rate among groups was compared with Chi-square. Little difference was found.

Table 8. Comparison of Friend Injury Witness during the War among Erenköy Turkish Cypriot Fighters and Turkish Cypriot Fighters

	Erenköy Turkish Cypriot Fighters		Turkish Cypriot Fighters		Total	
	N	%	N	%	N	%
Yes	49	98,0	47	94,0	96	96,0
No	1	2,0	3	6,0	4	4,0
Total	50	100,0	50	100,0	100	100,0

$\chi2= 1,042$, df=1, p=0,307 not answered=0

Both groups have witnessed high rate of friend being injured during the war.

Witness of friend injury among groups was compared with Chi-square. No any significant difference was found.

Table 9. Comparison of friend death witness during the war Among Erenköy Turkish Cypriot Fighters and Turkish Cypriot Fighters

	Erenköy Turkish Cypriot Fighters		Turkish Cypriot Fighters		Total	
	N	%	N	%	N	%
Yes	42	84,0	37	74,0	79	79,0
No	8	16,0	13	26,0	21	21,0
Total	50	100,0	50	100,0	100	100,0

$\chi2= 1,507$, df=1, p=0,220 not answered=0

Both groups have witnessed high rate of their friends being killed during the war, however rate of such if higher for Erenköy Cypriot Turkish Fighters.

Witness of friend death among groups was compared with Chi-square. No any significant difference was found.

Table 10. Comparison of Mental Readiness for War among Erenköy Turkish Cypriot Fighters and Turkish Cypriot Fighters

	Erenköy Turkish Cypriot Fighters		Turkish Cypriot Fighters		Total	
	N	%	N	%	N	%
Very prepared	2	4,0	20	40,0	22	22,0
Less prepared	2	4,0	12	24,0	14	14,0
Not prepared	46	92,0	18	36,0	64	64,0
Total	50	100,0	50	100,0	100	100,0

$\chi 2= 34,120$, df=2, p=0,000 not answered=0

Mental readiness for war was comparatively true for Turkish Cypriot Fighters, while for Erenköy Turkish Cypriot Fighters were not mentally prepared for war.

Mental readiness for war data was compared with Chi-square. A significant difference was found.

Table 11. Comparison of Degree of Expectancy of War among Erenköy Turkish Cypriot Fighters and Turkish Cypriot Fighters

	Erenköy Turkish Cypriot Fighters		Turkish Cypriot Fighters		Total	
	N	%	N	%	N	%
Expected	2	4,0	11	22,0	13	13,0
Less expected	1	2,0	12	24,0	13	13,0
Not expected	47	94,0	27	54,0	24	74,0
Total	50	100,0	50	100,0	100	100,0

$\chi2= 20,944$, df=2, p=0,000 not answered=0

While half of Turkish Cypriot Fighters were not expecting war, while almost every of Erenköy Turkish Cypriot Fighters were not expecting the war.

Degree of expectancy of war data compared with Chi-square. A significant difference was found.

Table 12. Comparison of commitment Level among Erenköy Turkish Cypriot Fighters and Turkish Cypriot Fighters

	Erenköy Turkish Cypriot Fighters		Turkish Cypriot Fighters		Total	
	N	%	N	%	N	%
High commitment	48	96,0	37	74,0	85	85,0
Low commitment	2	4,0	13	26,0	15	15,0
Total	50	100,0	50	100,0	100	100,0

$\chi2$= 9,757, df=2, p=0,008 not answered=0

Level of commitment for Erenköy Turkish Cypriot Fighters is about two times higher when compared to Turkish Cypriot Fighters.

Commitment level data were compared with Chi-square. A significant difference was found.

Table 13. Comparison of How the War Slogged Impacted Among Erenköy Turkish Cypriot Fighters and Turkish Cypriot Fighters

	Erenköy Turkish Cypriot Fighters		Turkish Cypriot Fighters		Total	
	N	%	N	%	N	%
It was easy to resist	1	2,0	8	16,0	9	9,0
It was not easy to resist	49	98,0	42	84,0	91	91,0
Total	50	100,0	50	100,0	100	100,0

$\chi2$= 37,644, df=2, p=0,000 not answered=0

War slogged impact rates are much higher for Erenköy Turkish Cypriot Fighters. War slogged impact data was compared with Chi-square. A significant difference was found.

Table 14. Comparison of Social Support during the War among Erenköy Turkish Cypriot Fighters and Turkish Cypriot Fighters

	Erenköy Turkish Cypriot Fighters		Turkish Cypriot Fighters		Total	
	N	%	N	%	N	%
Plenty	45	90,0	33	66,0	78	78,0
None	5	10,0	17	34,0	22	22,0
Total	50	100,0	50	100,0	100	100,0

$\chi2$= 8,392, df=1, p=0,004 not answered=0

Obtained data have shown that Erenköy Cypriot Turkish Fighters had more social support during the war period. Social support during the war data was compared with Chi-square. A difference was found.

Table 15. Comparison of Social Support Sources during the War among Erenköy Turkish Cypriot Fighters and Turkish Cypriot Fighters

	Erenköy Turkish Cypriot Fighters		Turkish Cypriot Fighters		Total	
	N	%	N	%	N	%
No one	2	4,0	9	18,0	11	11,0
Relatives	4	8,0	27	54,0	31	31,0
Friends	44	88,0	14	28,0	58	58,0
Total	50	100,0	50	100,0	100	100,0

$\chi2$= 37,036, df=2, p=0,000 not answered=0

Erenköy Turkish Cypriot Fighters received social support during the war mainly from their friends, while Turkish Cypriot Fighters received support mainly from their families. Social support sources during the war data was compared with Chi-square. A significant difference was found.

Table 16. Comparison of Present Educational Level among Erenköy Turkish Cypriot Fighters and Turkish Cypriot Fighters

	Erenköy Turkish Cypriot Fighters		Turkish Cypriot Fighters		Total	
	N	%	N	%	N	%
Non educated	0	0,0	14	28,0	14	14,0
Primary-High School	0	0,0	31	62,0	31	31,0
University	50	100,0	5	10,0	55	55,0
Total	50	100,0	50	100,0	50	100,0

$\chi 2$= 78,119, df=2, p=0,000 not answered=0

Present education of Erenköy Turkish Cypriot Fighters at the present day is University \graduates at least, while only minority of Turkish Cypriot Fighters graduated from University. Current educational level data was compared with Chi-square. A significant difference was found.

Table 17. Comparison of Present Marital Status among Erenköy Turkish Cypriot Fighters and Turkish Cypriot Fighters

Marital Status	Erenköy Turkish Cypriot Fighters		Turkish Cypriot Fighters		Total	
	N	%	N	%	N	%
Married	47	94,0	45	90,0	92	92,0
Widowed	3	6,0	5	10,0	8	8,0
Total	50	100,0	50	100,0	100	100,0

$\chi 2$= 0,543, df=1, p=, 461 not answered= 0

Marital status among both groups did not vary a lot, as majority of both groups participants are married. Current marital status data was compared with Chi-square. Not any significant difference was found.

Table 18. Comparison of Present Monthly Income Level among Erenköy Turkish Cypriot Fighters and Turkish Cypriot Fighters

Monthly income level	Erenköy Turkish Cypriot Fighters		Turkish Cypriot Fighters		Total	
	N	%	N	%	N	%
Medium	31	62,0	36	72,0	67	67,0
Good	19	38,0	14	28,0	33	33,0
Total	50	100,0	50	100,0	100	100,0

$\chi2$= 1,131, df=1, p=0,288 not answered= 0

Majority of both group participants have medium level of income, while difference among both groups does not differ dramatically. Current monthly income data was compared with Chi-square. Not any significant difference was found.

Table 19. Comparison of Disturbing Regret Feelings after the War among Erenköy Turkish Cypriot Fighters and Turkish Cypriot Fighters

	Erenköy Turkish Cypriot Fighters		Turkish Cypriot Fighters		Total	
	N	%	N	%	N	%
Yes	40	80,0	21	42,0	61	61,0
No	10	20,0	29	58,0	39	39,0
Total	50	100,0	50	100,0	100	100,0

$\chi2$= 15,174, df=1, p=0,000 not answered=0

Post war feeling of regret rate is twice higher among Erenköy Turkish Cypriot Fighters when compared to Turkish Cypriot Fighters. Disturbing regret data was compared with Chi-square. A significant difference was found.

Table 20. Comparison of War Impact among Erenköy Turkish Cypriot Fighters and Turkish Cypriot Fighters

	Erenköy Turkish Cypriot Fighters		Turkish Cypriot Fighters		Total	
	N	%	N	%	N	%
No impact	0	0,0	15	30,0	15	15,0
Low impact	7	14,0	16	32,0	23	23,0
High impact	43	86,0	19	38,0	62	62,0
Total	50	100,0	50	100,0	100	100,0

$\chi2$= 27,812, df=2, p=0,000 not answered=0

Impact of war for Erenköy Turkish Cypriot fighters is low impact for majority, while none said there is no impact of war. For Turkish Cypriot Fighters one third of group participants declared there was no war impact which significantly differ from Erenköy Turkish Cypriot Fighters.

Impact of war data was compared with Chi-square. A significant difference was found.

Table 21. Comparison of Increased Post-War Alcohol Consumption among Erenköy Turkish Cypriot Fighters and Turkish Cypriot Fighters

	Erenköy Turkish Cypriot Fighters		Turkish Cypriot Fighters		Total	
	N	%	N	%	N	%
Yes	15	30,0	9	18,0	24	24,0
No	35	70,0	41	82,0	76	76,0
Total	50	100,0	50	100,0	100	100,0

χ^2= 1,974, df=1, p=0,160 not answered=0

Both groups participants stated that increase in alcohol consumption have aroused during post-war period, however figures for Erenköy Turkish Cypriot Fighters is twice as much when compared to Turkish Cypriot Fighters.

Increased post-war alcohol consumption level data was compared with Chi-square. Very little significant difference was found.

Table 22. Comparison of Illegal psychoactive drug consumption in post-war period Among Erenköy Turkish Cypriot Fighters and Turkish Cypriot Fighters

	Erenköy Turkish Cypriot Fighters		Turkish Cypriot Fighters		Total	
	N	%	N	%	N	%
Yes	1	2,0	0	0,0	1	1,0
No	49	98,0	50	100,0	99	99,0
Total	50	100,0	50	100,0	100	100,0

χ^2= 1,010, df=1, p=0,315 not answered=0

Illegal psychoactive drug consumption was true for minority of Erenköy Turkish Cypriot Fighters while it was not the case for Turkish Cypriot Fighters. Illegal psychoactive drug consumption data was compared with Chi-square. No any significant difference was found.

Table 23. Comparison of Present alcohol consumption Among Erenköy Turkish Cypriot Fighters and Turkish Cypriot Fighters

	Erenköy Turkish Cypriot Fighters		Turkish Cypriot Fighters		Total	
	N	%	N	%	N	%
Yes	38	76,0	21	42,0	59	59,0
No	12	24,0	29	58,0	41	41,0
Total	50	100,0	50	100,0	100	100,0

$\chi2$= 11,947, df=1, p=0,001 not answered=0

Alcohol consumption rates at the moment of study were two times higher for Erenköy Turkish Cypriot Fighters. Present alcohol consumption data was compared with Chi-square. A significant difference was found.

Table 24. Comparison of PTSD Diagnosis Presence among Erenköy Turkish Cypriot Fighters and Turkish Cypriot Fighters

	Erenköy Turkish Cypriot Fighters		Turkish Cypriot Fighters		Total	
	N	%	N	%	N	%
No	26	52,0	47	94,0	73	73,0
Yes	24	48,0	3	6,0	27	27,0
Total	50	100,0	50	100,0	100	100,0

$\chi2$= 22,374, df=1, p=0,000 not answered=0

Presence of PTSD diagnosis among participants is higher for Erenköy Turkish Cypriot Fighters. PTSD diagnosis presence data compared with Chi-square. A significant difference was found.

Table 25. Comparison of Professional Help during Post-War Period among Erenköy Turkish Cypriot Fighters and Turkish Cypriot Fighters

	Erenköy Turkish Cypriot Fighters		Turkish Cypriot Fighters		Total	
	N	%	N	%	N	%
No	41	82,0	48	96,0	89	89,0
Physical Treatment	7	14,0	1	2,0	8	8,0
Psychiatry	2	4,0	1	2,0	3	3,0
Total	50	100,0	50	100,0	100	100,0

$\chi2$= 5,384, df=2, p=0,068 not answered=0

For Erenköy Turkish Cypriot Fighters professional treatment during post war period was times higher than among Cypriot Turkish Fighters. Post-war professional help data compared with Chi-square. No significant difference was found.

Table 26. Comparison of Post-War Social Support Levels among Erenköy Turkish Cypriot Fighters and Turkish Cypriot Fighters

	Erenköy Turkish Cypriot Fighters		Turkish Cypriot Fighters		Total	
	N	%	N	%	N	%
Plenty	20	40,0	27	54,0	47	47,0
Medium	21	42,0	12	24,0	33	33,0
None	9	18,0	11	22,0	20	20,0
Total	50	100,0	50	100,0	100	100,0

$\chi2$= 3,697, df=2, p=0,157 not answered=0

Turkish Cypriot Fighter has received more social support compared to Erenköy Turkish Cypriot Fighters. Post-war social support data compared with Chi-square. Very little significant difference was found.

Table 27. Comparison of Post-War Social Support Sources among Erenköy Turkish Cypriot Fighters and Turkish Cypriot Fighters

	Erenköy Turkish Cypriot Fighters		Turkish Cypriot Fighters		Total	
	N	%	N	%	N	%
No one	8	16,0	11	22,0	19	19,0
Relatives	13	26,0	35	70,0	48	48,0
Friends	16	32,0	4	8,0	20	20,0
Teachers	13	26,0	0	0,0	13	13,0
Total	50	100,0	50	100,0	100	100,0

$\chi2= 30,757$, df=3, p=0,000 not answered=0

While Turkish Cypriot Fighters received social support from relatives, while for Erenköy Turkish Cypriot Fighters main source of social support was friends. Post-war social support sources data compared with Chi-square. A significant difference was found.

Table 28. Comparison of Whether Difficulties Experienced During the War, Were Revealed To the Public Well Enough Among Erenköy Turkish Cypriot Fighters and Turkish Cypriot Fighters

	Erenköy Turkish Cypriot Fighters		Turkish Cypriot Fighters		Total	
	N	%	N	%	N	%
No	49	98,0	35	70,0	84	84,0
Yes	1	2,0	15	30,0	16	16,0
Total	50	100,0	50	100,0	100	100,0

$\chi2= 14,600$, df=2, p=0,001 not answered=0

Majority of both groups participants do not believe that difficulties experienced during the war are revealed to public well enough, yet such rate is higher for Erenköy Turkish Cypriot Fighters compared to Turkish Cypriot Fighters. Whether difficulties experienced during the war, were revealed to the public well enough data compared with Chi-square. A significant difference was found.

Table 29. Comparison of Financial support paid by government Among Erenköy Turkish Cypriot Fighters and Turkish Cypriot Fighters

	Erenköy Turkish Cypriot Fighters		Turkish Cypriot Fighters		Total	
	N	%	N	%	N	%
No	49	98,0	31	62,0	80	80,0
Yes	1	2,0	19	38,0	20	20,0
Total	50	100,0	50	100,0	100	100,0

$\chi2$= 20,250, df=1, p=0,000 not answered=0

Only one participant of Erenköy Turkish Cypriot Fighters group received some sort of support from government, while almost half of Turkish Cypriot Fighters received some financial support from government different among groups is clear. Financial support paid by government data compared with Chi-square. A significant difference was found.

Table 30.Comparison Of Non-Monetary Support Provided By Government Among Erenköy Turkish Cypriot Fighters And Turkish Cypriot Fighters

	Erenköy Turkish Cypriot Fighters		Turkish Cypriot Fighters		Total	
	N	%	N	%	N	%
No	48	96,0	45	90,0	93	93,0
Yes	2	4,0	5	10,0	7	7,0
Total	50	100,0	50	100,0	100	100,0

$\chi2$= 1,382, df=1, p=0,240 not answered=0

Majority of both group participants said they did not received any non-financial support from government. Non-monetary support provided by government data compared with Chi-square. Very little significant difference was found.

Table 31. Comparison of Expected compensation from government Among Erenköy Turkish Cypriot Fighters and Turkish Cypriot Fighters

	Erenköy Turkish Cypriot Fighters		Turkish Cypriot Fighters		Total	
	N	%	N	%	N	%
Had no expectations	44	88,0	12	24,05	56	56,0
Medal	6	12,0	26	52,0	32	32,0
Monetary	0	0,0	11	22,0	11	11,0
Recognition of Cyprus	0	0,0	1	2,0	1	1,0
Total	50	100,0	50	100,0	100	100,0

$\chi2= 42,786$, df=3, p=0,000 not answered=0

Majority of Erenköy Turkish Cypriot Fighters said they never expect any compensation from government, while almost half of Turkish Cypriot Fighters were expecting medal. Expected compensation from government data was compared with Chi-square. A significant difference was found.

Table 32. Comparison of Alcohol Consumption Frequency among Erenköy Turkish Cypriot Fighters and Turkish Cypriot Fighters

	Erenköy Turkish Cypriot Fighters		Turkish Cypriot Fighters		Total	
	N	%	N	%	N	%
No use	12	24,0	29	58,0	41	41,0
Everyday	5	10,0	1	2,0	6	6,0
Once a week	21	42,0	13	26,0	34	34,0
Once a month	12	24,0	7	14,0	19	19,0
Total	50	100,0	50	100,0	100	100,0

$\chi2= 12,914$, df=3, p=0,005 not answered=0

According to data obtained during research, alcohol consumption of Erenköy Turkish Cypriot Fighters is significantly higher than Turkish Cypriot Fighters. Alcohol consumption frequency data compared with Chi-square. A significant difference was found.

Table 33. Comparison of Will to quit drinking Among Erenköy Turkish Cypriot Fighters and Turkish Cypriot Fighters

	Erenköy Turkish Cypriot Fighters		Turkish Cypriot Fighters		Total	
	N	%	N	%	N	%
Doesn't consume alcohol	11	22,0	28	56,0	39	39,0
No	37	74,0	21	42,0	58	58,0
Yes	2	4,0	1	2,0	3	3,0
Total	50	100,0	50	100,0	100	100,0

$\chi2= 12,157$, df=2, p=0,002 not answered=0

Majority of Turkish Cypriot Fighters do not consume alcohol, while majority of Erenköy Turkish Cypriot Fighters consume alcohol and are not willing to quit alcohol consumption. Will to quiet drinking data compared with Chi-square. A significant difference was found.

Table 34. Comparison Of Being Criticized By Others Because Of Alcohol Consumption Among Erenköy Turkish Cypriot Fighters And Turkish Cypriot Fighters

	Erenköy Turkish Cypriot Fighters		Turkish Cypriot Fighters		Total	
	N	%	N	%	N	%
Doesn't consume alcohol	11	22,0	28	56,0	39	39,0
No	39	78,0	21	42,0	60	60,0
Yes	0	0,0	1	2,0	1	1,0
Total	50	100,0	50	100,0	100	100,0

$\chi2 = 13,810$, df=2, p=0,001 not answered=0

Majority of Erenköy Turkish Cypriot Fighters consume alcohol and none were critisized because of alcohol consumption. Only one participant of Turkish Cypriot Fighters was critisized because of alcohol consumption and majority of participants do not consume alcohol at all. Being criticized by others because of alcohol consumption data compared with Chi-square. A significant difference was found.

Table 35. Comparison of Feeling guilty for consumption of alcohol Among Erenköy Turkish Cypriot Fighters And Turkish Cypriot Fighters

	Erenköy Turkish Cypriot Fighters		Turkish Cypriot Fighters		Total	
	N	%	N	%	N	%
Doesn't consume alcohol	11	22,0	28	56,0	39	39,0
No	38	76,0	21	42,0	59	59,0
Yes	1	2,0	0	0	2	2,0
Total	50	100,0	50	100,0	100	100,0

$\chi2$= 12,309, df=2, p=0,002 not answered=0.

There are individuals feeling guilty for alcohol consumption among Erenköy Turkish Cypriot Fighters, as well as those who do not. However Turkish Cypriot Fighters are distributed into two opinions first is majority who does not consume alcohol at all and second are those who consume and do not feel any guilt for alcohol consumption. Feeling guilty for alcohol consumption data compared with Chi-square. A significant difference was found.

Table 36. Comparison Of Alcohol Consumption In The Morning Among Erenköy Turkish Cypriot Fighters And Turkish Cypriot Fighters

	Erenköy Turkish Cypriot Fighters		Turkish Cypriot Fighters		Total	
	N	%	N	%	N	%
Doesn't consume alcohol	11	22,0	28	56,0	39	39,0
No	37	74,0	22	44,0	59	59,0
Yes	2	4,0	0	0,0	2	2,0
Total	50	100,0	50	100,0	100	100,0%

$\chi2$= 13,224, df=2, p=0,001 not answered=0

As per information obtained during the study, none among Turkish Cypriot Fighters said that they consume alcohol in the morning, while few persons from Erenköy Turkish Cypriot Fighters admitted that they are consuming alcohol in the morning. Alcohol consumption in the morning data compared by Chi-square method. A significant difference was found.

Table 37. Comparison Presence of psychiatric disorders of relatives Among Erenköy Turkish Cypriot Fighters And Turkish Cypriot Fighters

	Erenköy Turkish Cypriot Fighters		Turkish Cypriot Fighters		Total	
	N	%	N	%	N	%
No	48	96,0	46	92,0	94	94,0
Anxiety disorder	0	0,0	1	2,0	1	1,0
Depression	1	2,0	3	6,0	4	4,0
Psychotic disorder	1	2,0	0	0,0	1	1,0
Total	50	100,0	50	100,0	100	100,0

$\chi^2= 3,043$, df=3, p=0,385 not answered=0

Presence of psychiatric disorders of relative's data compared with Chi-square. Very little significant difference was found.

In the scope of the present study, statistical analysis related to factors causing occurrence of PTSD. Significance of data obtained through questionnaires is primarily tested on by chi-square tests. Variables with interval validity of determined by chi-square were taken into binary logistic regression analysis.

In the present analysis PTSD was taken as a dependent variable, results of chi-square tests given in Table 38, which was made in order to obtain the relationship between dependent and independent variables.

Table 38. Relationship Between PTSD And Independent Variables of Both Erenköy Turkish Cypriot Fighters and Turkish Cypriot Fighters Who Has PTSD

Variables	Pearson Chi-Square	P
Pre-war education	96,222	0,000
Present education level	78,119	0,000
Military education period	41,230	0,000
War slogged impacted	37,644	0,000
Mental readiness	34,120	0,000
War impact	27,812	0,000
Expectancy of war	20,944	0,000
Financial support paid by government	20,250	0,000
Disturbing regret feelings	15,174	0,000
Difficulties during the war revealed to the public	14,600	0,001

In accordance with Chi-square significance tent results: Pre-war education (p=0,000), Present education level (p=0,000), Military education period (p=0,000), War slogged impacted (p=0,000), Mental readiness (p=0,000), War impact (p=0,000), Expectancy of war (p=0,000), Financial support paid by government (p=0,000), Disturbing regret feelings (p=0,000), Difficulties during the war revealed to the public (p=0,001) difference is significant. In other words, H_0 hypothesis supporting insignificance of PTSD presence and experience during pre-war, war and post-war periods is rejected. Therefore statistical significance of relationship between independent variables and PTSD diagnosis has been proven.

Binary logistic regression analysis mas made in order to estimate events triggering occurrence of PTSD and determine variables to be used during such estimation.

Results of Chi-square significance test which were determined as significant are used as independent variables of binary logistic regression analysis and are given in Table 38.

Herein for, variables affecting probability of PTSD diagnosis occurring due to war experience of Turkish Cypriot Fighters, PTSD diagnosis which is dependent variable and affecting it were determined.

Enter method is used to evaluate dependent variables of logistic regression analysis revealing PTSD diagnosis factors. β parameters and Wald statistics relative to such parameters, standard deviation, effect size and Exp (β) (ODDS) values are given in table 39.

Table 39. Logistic Regression Model. For Both Erenköy Turkish Cypriot Fighters and Turkish Cypriot Fighters With PTSD

Variables	B	Std. Dev.	Wald	df	p	Exp(β)
Constant	-97,303	16182,956	0,000	1	,995	0,000
Difficulties during the war revealed to the public	-1,861	1,525	1,488	1	0,001	0,156
Present education level	-1,821	1,262	2,082	1	0,000	0,162
Alcohol consumption	-1,319	1,027	1,651	1	0,000	0,267
Commitment	-0,428	0,497	0,740	1	0,000	0,652
Military rank	-0,403	1,454	0,077	1	0,000	0,668
Social support during the war	0,281	0,563	0,250	1	0,000	1,325
Military education period	0,317	2,421	0,017	1	0,000	1,374
War slogged impacted	0,322	0,600	0,288	1	0,000	1,380
Pre-war education	1,036	1,036	1,000	1	0,000	2,817
Financial support paid by government	1,749	2,709	,417	1	0,000	5,750

Significance of all independent variables causing PTSD diagnosis is shown in table 39. Exp (β) values in table 39 shows ODDS ratios. ODDS ratios reveal probability of appearance of one of two events observed relative to another, which may be shows as times less or times more. For results obtained β coefficient for some independent variables may be negative,

ODDS ratio could be interpreted as decreasing in scope of negative relationship. β ratio for several independent variables could be positive and therefore ODDS ratio shall be interpreted as increasing in accordance with positive relationship.

The validity of current model was examined by Hoshmer Lemeshow test.

Table 40. Erenköy Turkish Cypriot Fighters Chi-Square, PTSD Dependent Variable

Variable	Chi-square	P
Mental Readiness	8,333	0,004
Expectancy Of War	8,333	0,004
Disturbing Regret Feelings	7,41	0,006
Friend Death Witness	5,357	0,021
Friend Injury Rate	5,108	0,024

Table 41. Logistic Regression Model For Erenköy Turkish Cypriot Fighters With PTSD

	B	S.E.	Wald	df	Sig.	Exp(B)
Constant	-22,472	25779,903	,000	1	,999	,000
Friend Death Witness	-1,209	1,043	1,345	1	,246	,298
Expectancy Of War	,302	4985,185	,000	1	1,000	1,353
Friend Injury Rate	1,656	,942	3,091	1	,079	5,237
Disturbing Regret Feelings	1,943	,982	3,912	1	,048	6,977
Mental Readiness	11,001	12889,952	,000	1	,999	59935,682

Table 42. Turkish Cypriot Fighters Chi-Square, PTSD Dependent Variable

Variable	Chi-square	P
Mental Readiness	9,722	0,002
Expectancy Of War	6,044	0,014
Difficulties Experienced During The War Revealed To Public	11,017	0,026
Presence Of Mental Illness In Pre-War Period	4,861	0,027
Military Rank	3,431	0,064

Table 43. Logistic Regression Model. For Turkish Cypriot Fighters With PTSD

	B	S.E.	Wald	Df	Sig.	Exp(B)
Constant	-,336	15529,198	,000	1	1,000	,714
Military Rank	-20,511	9476,419	,000	1	,998	,000
Difficulties Experienced During The War Revealed To Public	-,118	,928	,016	1	,899	,889
Expectancy Of War	,302	4985,185	,000	1	1,000	1,353
Presence Of Mental Illness In Pre-War Period	10,120	4847,342	,000	1	,998	24824,584
Mental Readiness	10,173	5227,953	,000	1	,998	26176,006

4. DISCUSSION

In the present study, severity and presence of PTSD among Turkish Cypriot Fighters and Erenköy Turkish Cypriot Fighters were evaluated.

Level of PTSD determined among Erenköy Turkish Cypriot Fighters is: 48 % and for Turkish Cypriot Fighters is 6%. Study was carried 40 years after the war. Majority of studies related to post-war PTSD strengthen hypothesis that PTSD remains present even 30-50 years after the war (Ikin, et.al. 2007), (Favaro A. et.al., 1999, 87-95), (Blanchard MS, et.al. 2006). After a traumatic event, many individuals may experience some of PTSD symptoms; for most of them, these symptoms may naturally decrease over time. However sometimes symptoms may persist. Even though, symptoms may not be severe enough to meet criteria for a PTSD diagnosis, they can still interfere with individual's life. In addition, if symptoms are not adequately addressed, those could increase risk for delayed-onset PTSD. (Averill, et.al. 2000, 84-88). Kulka and friends have stated that PTSD symptoms prevalence at Vietnam War veterans was calculated as 31% and up to 70% at those who participated in most violent clashes, even 30 years after the war. (Kulka R.A. et al., 1990). As they have stated about half of those Vietnam veterans who have ever had PTSD, would still have it today (around 30 years post-trauma) (Kessler R.A., et.al. 1995). Within the key frame of the study made with veterans have shown that majority of PTSD symptoms are seen during lifetime. Lifetime prevalence rate of PTSD at World War II veterans is 18, 5%; while another study indicated rate of 27%. (Blake D, et.al., 1990, 15-27), (Rosen J, et al, 1989, 65-69). In studies made with Vietnam War fighters have shown PTSD prevalence rate range of 14-30% for white, Afro-Americans 19-47%, and 28% for Latin (Marsella A.J., et. al. 1993, 157-181).

Klutznik and his friends have stated that PTSD symptoms severity would decrease through the time, whereas affective disorders, generalized anxiety and alcohol abuse frequency would increase. (Kluznik J, et al, 1986, 1443-1446). Feeling of estrangement appears at elderly age and alienation from youth is observed. Under such circumstances in order to maintain self-esteem a person will take refuge in the past and begins to reconsider memories. During such memories rethinking, traumatic ones would revive and cause increase of depression, anxiety and feeling of hopelessness. (Sadavoy J, 1994, 19-26). Most critical factor related to PTSD development is traumatic event itself. (March J.S., 1990, 61-82). As seen from this study, Erenköy battle event is very traumatic itself, and it affect more and worse. Erenköy Turkish Cypriot Fighters are more likely to use alcohol, guilty feelings and during feeling questionnaires were more likely to express negative feelings about the Erenköy battle, about the period they were in Erenköy.

Comparison of injury occurrence among Erenköy Turkish Cypriot Fighters and Turkish Cypriot Fighters during the war period: Erenköy Turkish Cypriot Fighters experienced life threating injury, injury which required outpatient treatment; while less of Turkish Cypriot Fighters experienced life threating injury, injury which requires outpatient treatment. Absence of military education and experience may cause more frequent occurrence of life threating injures among Erenköy Turkish Cypriot Fighters.

Disturbing regret feelings distribution among Erenköy Turkish Cypriot Fighters is as: 42% and Turkish Cypriot Fighters: 80%. Majority of participants, believe that they have done all that they can, and they have done their best, in order to protect their motherland.

Individuals exposed to traumatic events, such as war, experience moral injury which is experience likely provoking such feelings as mild or intense grief, shame, guilt, sorrow and regret. Because during the war believes collapse and the war causes impact wounds, resulting in moral injury. Vietnam veterans reported that they are far from regretting of that time and all said that they are very proud of what they have made. (Watkins J.R. 2011).

It is noteworthy that individuals whom had drug or alcohol abuse in the past are more likely to start using those again in order to decrease anxiety as well as those who passed through anxiety or depression would eventually exhibit such symptoms again (Solomon Z. 1988, 323–329). Post war alcohol consumption has increased for Fighters and such has reached higher levels for Erenköy Turkish Cypriot Fighters when compared to increase of consumption for Turkish Cypriot Fighters.

Rate of current alcohol use for Erenköy Turkish Cypriot Fighters is prevailing as well. Study has shown that Erenköy Turkish Cypriot Fighters consume alcohol more frequently too. As it is seen from the result of study, Erenköy Turkish Cypriot Fighters who has a higher level of PTSD, are more likely to use alcohol in order to have relief of symptoms as anxiety, depression and regret feelings. And consumption frequency is more often than at Turkish Cypriot Fighters. Even though, Erenköy Turkish Cypriot Fighters are more willing to quit alcohol compared to Turkish Cypriot Fighters. Erenköy Turkish Cypriot Fighters are less likely to admit that they were criticized because of their alcohol consumption and feeling guilty as per alcohol consumption is less likely to be reported by Erenköy Turkish Cypriot Fighters. Conducted alcohol use intake in the mornings is more likely to be reality for Erenköy Turkish Cypriot Fighters.

Chronicity of PTDS was seen during setting the diagnosis for Erenköy Turkish Cypriot Fighters and Turkish Cypriot Fighters. Though they experience some symptoms even after 40 years of war. And mostly the participants of that study, report that symptoms started 12 months after returning from war. According to Erenköy Turkish Cypriot Fighters, they had to settle up their lives again, turn back to school, arrange their homes, dormidortories, etc. This may affect the onset of PTSD symptoms – as seen the delayed onset of PTSD in Erenköy Turkish Cypriot Fighters.

As a result of the study education level before war among Turkish Cypriot Fighters and Erenköy Turkish Cypriot Fighters, the difference between education levels were revealed, in pre-war period all of Erenköy Turkish Cypriot Fighters were university students. While Turkish Cypriot Fighters were mostly primary-high school educated. Level of education is a factor of coping with PTSD as well. PTSD prevalence at any moment in a lifetime will significantly decrease as level of education is growing (Breslau N, et.al., 1991, 216-222).

Level of education is associated with PTSD symptoms, both may cause and consequence, as individuals with lower level of educational are more likely to be exposed to traumas and obtain high PTSD symptoms. (Priebe S, et.al. 2009, 393-397).
The results of another study have proved that level of education has no impact on PTSD vulnerability. (Sana R, et.al. 2014, 27-32). In this scope, results obtained in present research, can postulate that Erenköy Turkish Cypriot Fighters higher level of education and high PTSD level can be explained. Fighters were university students before they came to Erenköy Exclave. And the education level of Turkish Cypriot Fighters did not increased during the post war period based on negative experience.

Researches made with individuals exposed to trauma in younger age, especially adolescents show that, for youngsters and elderly individuals it is harder to cope with trauma when compared to middle age individuals. (Breslau N. et.al., 1992, 671-675), (Resnick H.S. et.al., 1989, 860-866), (Solomon Z. 1988, 323–329). However the Erenköy Turkish Cypriot Fighters were university students abroad, and therefore they didn't realize the war in reality as opposed to Turkish Cypriot Fighters, whom lived during beginning of crisis in early stages of war. And were informed about all incidents occurring in their motherland, people were waiting with their guns at home every day, and expecting war to happen. Which reveals the fact that war wasn't sudden, and was expected by those who lived in Cyprus at close prewar period? This couldn't be said to Erenköy Turkish Cypriots, who were abroad and had no any information about crisis. Because media was very insufficient, and they were not able to get any information from Cyprus. They had learned about the beginning of war, very soon. Above mentioned facts reveal extreme level of unexpectancy of war among Erenköy Turkish Cypriot Fighters as majority did not expected war, when compared to Turkish Cypriot Fighters whom had military training and were mentally prepared for probability of war. As well one of the most common factors of mental preparation of fighters is special military education. As revealed in this study that majority of Turkish Cypriot Fighters passed through long-termed military education, while Erenköy Turkish Cypriot Fighters had chance of military education for only few weeks after the war have started and some had no any military education.

Military ranking is also an important factor which affects level of traumatic exposure of individuals. Military rank level difference among Erenköy Turkish Cypriot Fighters and Turkish Cypriot Fighters was not major. Difference of commander rank determination among Erenköy Turkish Cypriot Fighters was based on personal leadership skills and other personality qualities, while among Turkish Cypriot Fighters, commander was determined in accordance with military order considering level of military education, and years of service in army and Turkish Resistance Organization. Many studies show that lack of military education is likely to develop PTSD. (Hendin H. et.al., 1991, 586-591). As mentioned above Turkish Cypriot Fighters include professional soldiers with years of service, which clearly understood how they shall commit their duties in order to conclude their military duties. But Erenköy Turkish Cypriot Fighters were students full of enthusiasm but had little or no military skills, sincerely willing to risk their lives and do what it takes to defend their motherland. Those facts reveal difference among both groups mindset during the war. The high commitment levels of Erenköy Turkish Cypriot Fighters exceed those measured for Turkish Cypriot Fighters.

The War impact had higher amplitude among Erenköy Turkish Cypriot Fighters when compared to Turkish Cypriot Fighters. High level of war impact among Erenköy Turkish Cypriot Fighters was triggered by such factors as: inability to communicate with relatives and outer world which led to confusions about strategic objectives, insufficient knowledge about territory of Erenköy Exclave. Geographical features of exclave itself eliminating group from friendly armed forces which made them feel being left alone on their only destiny. Lack of ammunition, absence of food and water for many weeks, proper clothes, medications and any medical aid. Decreased their ability to resist their enemies. A person must experience "fear, helplessness or horror" in reaction to a trauma   or environmental stressor. Many military personnel don't experience those reactions because they are trained to handle adverse events.

Permanence of psychological diseases developed after trauma is invasively proportional to the level of social support provided to individual. (Burgess A.W. et.al., 1979, 648-657). In our study levels of social support during the war were evaluated as those are important factors of PTSD development. Majority of social support received during the war among Erenköy Turkish Cypriot Fighters is plenty support and among Turkish Cypriot Fighters plenty support received was a major value, however lower when compared to Erenköy Turkish Cypriot

Fighters. Information obtained have shown that social support provided to Erenköy Turkish Cypriot Fighters during the war sourced from close friends, which they become to each other during period of war. They were cut off from outer world, remaining under same circumstances triggered them mutually fulfill need of social support. However, Turkish Cypriot Fighters had a chance to interact with their families, relatives and community they belonged.

Interpretations vary depending on secondary support systems level and social burden of trauma: social support retains individual from unforeseen secondary trauma. It is important to distinguish safety and danger and spotting danger in supporting environment would help regain psychological balance. In another words, traumatized individuals recovery in post-traumatic supportive environment would be easier. Development of PTSD denotes deficit of social support. In such a manner traumatic experience information processed with interruptions on cognitive level. Secondary trauma occurring affect post-traumatic conformity. That leads to inhibition of manifestation and expression of trauma, causes unhealthy and unbeneficial change as well as emerges ever growing anger. Social support levels after war among both groups seem not very much, however, Erenköy Turkish Cypriot Fighters were immediately send back abroad, where from they came to fight, and they were restricted to come back to Cyprus, for a long period of time. Those facts reveal significance of support sources among both groups where Erenköy Turkish Cypriot Fighters were not able to receive social support from their relatives or government and again had to support each other. Significant source of support study has spotted were teachers at universities which allowed them to continue their education, despite that they left their schools, without any official permission. And therefore support provided by teachers could not be equal to support provided by relatives to Turkish Cypriot Fighters.

Traumatic events with no doubt will always effect social life of the person. Social reaction during and after the traumatic event plays a decisive role when it comes to psychological problems caused by the event. While support of surrounding people would decrease effect of traumatic event, unfriendly and negative attitude increases severity of trauma. (Flannery R.B. Jr., et.al., 1990, 415-420). Support at early post- traumatic stages, helps to restore confidence. Solidarity and mutual commitment among the group during the war have proven to keep individuals from trauma.

Prerequisite of seeing world more meaningful is ability to share traumatic event with other people. During that period a person would look for support not only from first had relatives, but overall surrounding society. Society to which individual belongs plays an important role in resolving of the trauma. Remedy of a gap between individual and society primarily depends on acceptance of the event by society and then on society behavior related to the event. When society accepts the fact that individual has been traumatized, feeling responsible leads to remedy endeavor. Two types of social response are required to relieve traumatization of the individual and those are awareness and effort for curing. At post-war periods those are ensured through acceptance of significance of the war by the civil population as well as elation of war veterans.

Turkish Cypriot Fighters are mostly recognized and appreciated as fighters and heroes in the public. While deeds of Erenköy Turkish Cypriot Fighters remain undervalued and are not recognized enough.

In opinions of majority of Erenköy Turkish Cypriot Fighters groups participants recognition level of difficulties experienced during the war were not revealed well enough, while among Turkish Cypriot Fighters yet majority has the same opinion, however for Turkish Cypriot Fighters such a majority includes lesser participants when compared to Erenköy Turkish Cypriot Fighters.

In a post war period monetary and non-monetary support provided by government significantly differs among both groups: for Erenköy Turkish Cypriot Fighters which received financial support paid by government conclude insignificant minority while for Other Turkish Cypriot Fighters those figures are almost half of participants. North Cyprus government has provided point system for Turkish Cypriot Fighters which allowed them to obtain property in North Cyprus in accordance of military service period. However Erenköy Turkish Cypriot Fighters were not given such points. Also majority of Turkish Cypriot Fighters were serving for government before the war, and in post war period, gain prioritized retirement status. While Erenköy Turkish Cypriot Fighters were students and didn't serve for government, accordingly were not included in prioritized retirement.
And non-monetary support figures among groups don't differ much. But expectations among groups are different. Majority of Erenköy Turkish Cypriot Fighters had no any expectations

from government, while Turkish Cypriot Fighters mainly expected medal and monetary compensation.

5. ERENKÖY SYNDROME

Current study states that, Erenköy Turkish Cypriot Fighters have a higher rate of PTSD. Such is related to Cyprus War, namely Erenköy Enclave Battle. This condition left them invasive memories, nightmares, flashbacks, loss of concentration, survivor guilt feelings, sleep disturbances and alcohol consumption. The main distinctive characteristic of Erenköy Enclave Battle is that fighters mainly consisted of young university students and those came to protect their motherland as the matter of their own will and no government recruited them. Those young boys struggled during two years at Erenköy Enclave with no government help or support.

Finally despite all inflictions they have passed through, they were sent to Turkish Republic by government. At their arrival, they were qualified by public not as heroes risking their lives, but as useless and unnecessary. They receive no guerdon.

Criterions of Erenköy Syndrome are distributed in two groups:

Conditions special to Erenköy War:

- Extremely unexpected situation
- To be an adolescent
- Absence or insufficient military education
- To be exposed to severe life threatening and injury
- Not easy to resist war atmosphere
- Social support only among themselves
- Lifelong negative impact of war
- Absence of mental readiness

Psychological symptoms:

- Feelings of hopelessness and disappointment
- Feeling strong without any expectations
- Disturbing regret feelings
- Feelings of not being understood

6. CONCLUSION

As a result of the present study even after long period of time PTSD symptoms can be found. Furthermore, a study has shown that special conditions of war can cause endemic psychological complaints.

"Normal young boys were taken out of their offices and factories and classrooms and put into the ranks. There they were made over; they were made to face, to regard murder as the daily activity. They were put shoulder to shoulder and, through mass psychology, they entirely changed. They were trained and made think that they kill or would be killed. Those boys in the post war period now need to face another reality and accept killing as anti-social deed as it was normal for them years ago. However all those experiences do not simply evaporate and disappear. Years spent with "kill or be killed" mindset. And now those mature boys had to deal with their problems on their own. Readjustment after years of mass psychology trainings and dramatic experiences is never easy, and it was harder especially for them. Society didn't need them anymore. So they were scattered without any speeches or parades.

Many, too many, of these fine young boys are eventually destroyed, mentally, because they could not make that final mindset readjustment on their own.

REFERENCES

Adler A, Neuropsychiatric Complications In Victims Of Boston's Coconut Grove Disaster, **JAMA** 123 (1943): 1098–1101.

Aker A.T., Özeren M., Başoğlu M., Cem, CAPS-1 Turkish Form Reliability And Validity Study, **Turkish Journal Of Psychiatry** 10 (1999):286-293.

American Heritage Dictionary: War. Thefreedictionary.Com. Access Date 25.01.2014.
American Psychiatric Association (APA). **Diagnostic and statistical manual of mental disorders, third edition. (DSM-I)**, Washington, DC, American Psychiatric Press, (1952)

American Psychiatric Association (APA). **Diagnostic and statistical manual of mental disorders, third edition. (DSM-II)**, Washington, DC, American Psychiatric Press, (1968)

American Psychiatric Association (APA). **Diagnostic and statistical manual of mental disorders, third edition. (DSM-III)**, Washington, DC, American Psychiatric Press, (1980); 238.

American Psychiatric Association. (APA). **Diagnostic and statistical manual of mental disorder, third edition revised (DSM-III-R)**, Washington, DC, American Psychiatric Press, (1987): 247-251.

American Psychiatric Association (APA). **Diagnostic and statistical manual of mental disorders, fourth edition. (DSM-IV)**, Washington, DC, American Psychiatric Press, (1994): 424-429.

Andreasen, N.J.C. Posttraumatic Stress Disorder. **Comprehensive Textbook Of Psychiatry**, Vol IV. Edited By Kaplan HI, Sadock BJ. Baltimore, Williams & Wilkins, (1985):918–924.

Averill, P.M., & Beck, J.G. Posttraumatic stress disorder of older adults: A conceptual review. **Journal of Anxiety Disorders**, 14, (2000): 133-156

Bahadır M. **"Girne-Baf-Limasol ve Larnaka Katliamları"** Genç Mücahitler Dernegi Yayınları (2013):84-88

Basoglu, M., Mineka, A., Paker, M., Aker, T., Livanou, M., & Gok, S. Psychological Preparedness For Trauma As A Protective Factor In Survivors Of Torture. **Psychological Medicine**, 27 (1997): 1421–1433.

BBC Article On This Day 10 August 1964
Http://News.Bbc.Co.Uk/Onthisday/Hi/Dates/Stories/August/10/Newsid_3037000/3037898. Stm Access Date 25.01.2014.

Blake D, Keane T, Wine P, et.al.., Prevalence Of Post-Traumatic Stress Disorder Symptoms In Combat Veterans Seeking Medical Treatment. *Journal of* **Traumatic** *Stress*, 3(1990):15-27.

Brady, K.T., Back, S.E., & Coffey, S.F. Substance abuse and posttraumatic stress disorder. **Current Directions in Psychological Science**, (2004). 13, 206-209.

Breslau N, Davis GC, Andreski P, Peterson Foa EB, Trauma And Women: Course, Predictors And Treatment. **Journal of Clinical Psychiatry** 5 (Suppl 9) (1997): 25-28.

Breslau N, Davis GC, Andreski P. Traumatic Events And PTSD In An Urban Population Of Young Adults. **Archives Of General Psychiatry** 48 (1991): 216-222.

Breslau N, Davis GC, Posttraumatic Stres Disorder In An Urban Population Of Young Adults: Risk Factors For Chronicity, **American Journal of Psychiatry**, 149 (1992):671-675.

Breslau, N., Davis, G. C., & Andreski, P., Risk Factors For PTSD-Related Traumatic Events: A Prospective Analysis. **American Journal Of Psychiatry**, 152(1995):529–535.

Breslau, N., Kessler, R. C., Chilcoat, H. D., Schultz, L. R., Davis, G. C., & Andreski, P., Trauma And Posttraumatic Stress Disorder In The Community: Detroit Area Survey Of Trauma. **Archives Of General Psychiatry**,55 (1998):626–632.

Brewin, C. R., Andrews, B., & Valentine, J. D., Meta-Analysis Of Risk Factors For Posttraumatic Stress Disorder In Trauma Exposed Adults. **Journal Of Consulting And Clinical Psychology**, 68 (2000):748–766.

Brewin, C. R., Intrusive Autobiographical Memories In Depression And Post-Traumatic Stress Disorder. **Applied Cognitive Psychology**, 12 (1998):359–370.

Bryant, R.A., & Harvey, A.G. . Posttraumatic stress in volunteer fighters: Predictors of distress. **Journal of Nervous and Mental Disease**, 183, (1995)267-271.

Burgess AW, Holmstrom LL. Rape: sexual disruption and recovery. **American Journal of Orthopsychiatry** 49(4) (1979): 648-657.

Burstein A. Posttaumatic stress disorder. **Journal of Clinical Psychiatry**; 46(7) (1985):300-301.

Carlson E.B., Rosser-Hogan R.Y., Tauma Experiences, Posttraumatic Stress, Dissociation And Depression In Cambodian Refugees. **American Journal of Psychiatry**, 148 (1991):1548-1551.

Clausewitz C. V., Howard M., Paret P., **"Eds. On War"**, Princenton University Press (1984): 428-465.

Cole PM, Putnam FW. Effect of incest on self and social functioning: a developmental psychopathology perspective. Journal of Consulting Clinical Psychology; 60(2) (1992): 174-184.

Corneil, W., Beaton, R., Murphy, S., Johnson, C., & Pike, K.. Exposure to traumatic incidents and prevalence of posttraumatic stress symptomatology in urban fighters in two countries. **Journal of Occupational Health Psychology**, 4, (1999) 131-141.

Davidson J. Issues in the diagnosis of posttraumatic stress disorder. **Review of Psychiatry** **12** (1993): 141-155.

Davidson J.R.T.,Hughes D.,Blazer D.G., George L.K., PTSD In The Community: An Epidemiological Study, **Psychological Medicine**, 21 (1991):713-721.

Del Ben, K.S., Scotti, J.R., Chen, Y., & Fortson, B.L. Prevalence of posttraumatic stress disorder symptoms in firefighters. **Work and Stress**, 20, (2006). 37-48.

Ehlers A, Mayou RA, Bryant B. Psychological Predictors Of Chronic Posttraumatic Stress Disorder After Motor Vehicle Accidents. **Journal of Abnormal Psychology**, 107 (3) (1998): 508-519.

Encyclopaedia-Britannica Http://Www.Britannica.Com/Ebchecked/Topic/628478/Vietnam-War Access Date 25.01.2014

Favaro A., F. C. Rodella, G. Colombo And P. Santonastaso Post-Traumatic Stress Disorder And Major Depression Among Italian Nazi Concentration Camp Survivors: A Controlled Study 50 Years Later. **Psychological Medicine**, 29, (1999) 87-95.

Flannery R. From victim to survivor: a stress management approach in the treatment of learned helplessness. Van der Kolk (ed.). Psychological trauma. Washington, DC, **American Psychiatric Press**, (1987): 217-232.

Flannery RB Jr, Flannery GJ. Sense of coherence, life stress, and psychological distress: a prospective methodological inquiry. **Journal of Clinical Psychology** 46(4) (1990) 415-420.

Foa EB, Trauma and Women: Course, Predictors and Treatment, **Journal of Clinical Psychiatry**, 5 (Suppl 9) (1997): 25-28.

Friedman M.J., Keane T.M., Resick P.A., **"Handbook of PTSD: Science and Practice"** New York Gulford Press (2nd ed.) (2007).

Friedman, M.J., Post-Vietnam Syndrome: Recognition and Management. **The Academy of Psychosomatic Medicine** 22, No. 11 (1981): 931-943.

Frye JS, Stockton RA. Discriminant analysis of posttraumatic stress disorder among a group of Vietnam veterans. **American Journal of Psychiatry** 139(1) (1982): 52-56.

Garland C: The Lasting Trauma Of The Concentration Camp. **BMJ**, 307 (1993):77-78.

Glass A.J., Jones F.D. "Psychiatry In The U.S. Army: Lessons For Community Psychiatry" Uniformed Services University of The Health Sciences Medicine. **Military National Government Publication** (2005).

Goenjian A.K., Armen K., Louis M., et.al.. PTSD In Elderly And Younger Adults After The 1988 Earthquake In Armenia. **American Journal of Psychiatry**, 151(6) (1994):895-901.

Gray MJ, Bolton EE, Litz BT , A longitudinal analysis of PTSD symptom course: Delayed-onset PTSD in Somalia peacekeepers. **J Consult Clinical Psychology** (2004) 72(5):909–913

Green BL, Grace MC, Vary MG Et. Al. Children Of Disaster In The Second Decade: A 17-Year Follow-Up Of Buffalo Creek Survivors. **Journal of The American Academy of Child and Adolescent Psychiatry** (1994) , 33: 71-79

Green BL, Lindy JD, Grace MC Et.al.. Chronic PTSD And Diagnostic Comorbidity In A Disaster Sample, **Journal of Nervous and Mental Disease** (1992) 180: 760-766

Green MA, Berlin MA. Five psychosocial variables related to the existence of post-traumatic stress disorder symptoms. **Journal of Clinical Psychology** 43(6) (1987): 643-649.

Güleç, C., Köroğlu E. **Psikiyatri Temel Kitabı**, Ankara: Hekimler Yayın Birliği, (1997).

Harter S, Alexander PC, Neimeyer RA. Long-term effects of incestuous child-abuse in college-women: social adjustment, social cognition, and family characteristics. **Journal Consult Clinical Psychology** 56(1): 1988; 5-8.

Haslam, C., & Mallon, K.. A preliminary investigation of posttraumatic stress symptoms among fighters. **Work and Stress**, 17, (2003) 277-285.

Helzer J, Robins L, McEvoy L. PTSD in general population: Findings of the epidemiologic catchment area survey. **N Eng J Med** 1987; 317(26): 1630-1634.

Helzer, John E.; Robins, Lee N.; And Mcevoy, Larry.. PTSD In The General Population. **The New England Journal Of Medicine** 317, No. 26: (1987) 1630-1634.

Hendin H, Haas AP. Suicide and guilt as manifestations of PTSD in Vietnam combat veterans. **Am J Psychiatry** (1991); 148(5):586-591.

HENDIN, H., & HAAS, A. P. Suicide and guilt as manifestations of posttraumatic stress disorder in Vietnam veterans. **American Journal of Psychiatry**, (1991), 586-591.

Henn, Francis "A Business Of Some Heat: The United Nations Force In Cyprus 1972-74", Pen & Sword Military (2004): 240-360.

Herman JL. **A new diagnosis. In Trauma and recovery**. New York: Basic Books, (1992): 115-129.

Howell S.,Willis R., 'To Be Angry Is Not To Be Human, But To Be Fearful Is": Chewong Concepts of Human Nature." **In Societies at Peace: Anthropological Perspectives,** London and New York: Routledge, (1989): 45-59.

Huppenbauer, Sandra L. November PTSD: A Portrait Of The Problem. **American Journal Of Nursing** 82, No. 11(1982):1699-1703.

J. Richard Watkins '**Vietnam: No Regrets: One Soldier's "Tour of Duty**" State Publishing; 2nd edition (2011)

Jacobsen, L. K., Southwick, S. M., & Kosten, T. R. , Substance Use Disorders In Patients With Posttraumatic Stress Disorder: A Review Of The Literature. **American Journal Of Psychiatry,** 158, (2001):1184–1190.

Johnson JG, Cohen P, Brown J, Smailes EM, Bernstein DP. Childhood maltreatment increases risk for personality disorders during early adulthood. **Arch Gen Psychiatry** (1999); 56(7): 600-606.

Jordan, B. K., Marmar, C. R., Fairbank, J. A., Schlenger, W. E., Kulka, R. A., Hough, R. L., et al. Problems in families of male Vietnam Veterans with posttraumatic stress disorder. **Journal of Consulting and Clinical Psychology**, 60, (1992), 916-926.
Jordan, B. K., Schlenger, W. E., Hough, R. L., Kulka, R. A., Weiss, D. S., Fairbank, J. A., et al. Lifetime and current prevalence of specific psychiatric disorders among Vietnam Veterans and controls. **Archives of General Psychiatry**, 48, (1991), 207-215.

Kang HK, Natelson BH, Mahan CM, et al. Post-traumatic stress disorder and chronic fatigue syndrome-like illness among Gulf War veterans: a population-based survey of 30,000 veterans. **Am J Epidemiol** (2003); 157:141–8.

Karalı N, Yüksel Ş. Effects of forced migration on psychological problems seen after torture. **Serbest bildiri. Fifth European Conference on Traumatic Stress:** (1997) 29 June-3 July, Maastrich.

Kaylor JA, King DV, King LA. Psychological effects of military service in Vietnam: A meta-analysis. **Psychol Bull** (1987); 102(2): 257-271.

Keane TM, Scott WO, Chavoya GA, Lamparski DM, Fairbank JA.Social support in Vietnam veterans with posttraumatic stress disorder: A comparative analysis. **J Consult Clin Psychol** (1985); 53(1): 95-102.

Keegan J., "A History Of Warfare" Pimlico (2004): 1-61.

Keser, Ulvi **Kıbrıs'ta Yeraltı Faaliyetleri ve Türk Mukavemet Teşkilatı**. IQ Kültür-Sanat Yayınları, Istanbul, (2007):640

Kessler, R. C., Sonnega, A., Bromet, E., Hughes, M., & Nelson, C. B. Posttraumatic Stress Disorder In The National Comorbidity Survey. **Archives Of General Psychiatry**, 52 (1995): 1048-1060.

Kıbrıs Türk Milli Mücadelesi ve Bu Mücadelede TMT'nin Yeri, Cilt I, Lefkoşa (2009) s. VI.

Kilpatrick D, Saunders B, Amick-McMullen A., Best,CL, Veronen LJ, Resnick HS. Victim and crime factors associated with the development of post-traumatic stress disorder. **Behavior Therapy** (1989); 20: 199-214.

King, D. W., King, L. A., Fairbank, J. A., Keane, T. M., & Adams, G.. Resilience-recovery factors in posttraumatic stress disorder among female and male Vietnam Veterans: Hardiness, postwar social support, and additional stressful life events. **Journal of Personality and Social Psychology**, (1998) 74, 420-434.

King, D. W., King, L. A., Foy, D. W., & Gudanowski, D. M.. Prewar factors in combat-related posttraumatic stress disorder: Structural equation modeling with a national sample of female and male Vietnam Veterans .**Journal of Consulting and Clinical Psychology**, (1996) 64, 520-531.

King, D. W., King, L. A., Foy, D. W., Keane, T. M., & Fairbank, J. A.. Posttraumatic stress disorder in a national sample of female and male Vietnam Veterans: Risk factors, war-zone stressors, and resilience-recovery variables. **Journal of Abnormal Psychology**, (1999)108, 164-170.

King, D. W., King, L. A., Gudanowski, D. M., & Vreven, D. L. Alternative representations of war zone stressors: Relationships to posttraumatic stress disorder in male and female Vietnam Veterans. **Journal of Abnormal Psychology**, (1995) 104, 184-196.

Kinzey J.D. Boehnlein J.K. Leung P.K. Et.al., The Prevalence Of PTSD And Its Clinical Significance Among Southeast Asian Refugees. **American Journal of Psychiatry** 147 (1990) 913-917.

Kluznik J, Speed N Van Valkenberg C Et Al: Forty-Year Follow-Up of United States Prisoners Of War. **American Journal of Psychiatry** (1986): 1443-1446.

Koken R. "Memoirs **Of A Cypriot Of '64 Generation**" Basak Press (2012): 129-144, 111-117.

Koopman C, Classen C, Spiegel D: Predictors Of Posttraumatic Stress Symptoms Among Survivors Of The Oakland/Berkeley, Calif, **Firestorm. American Journal of Psychiatry** 151(1994):888–894.

Kotak I. "**Şu Bizim Kıbrıs – I Unutulan Tarihin Gerçekleri**" Ajans Press 2012

Kulka RA, Schlenger WE, Fairbank JA et.al. **The National Vietnam Veterans Readjustment Study: Tables of findings and technical appendices.** New York: Brunner/Mazel., (1990a).

Kulka, R. A., Schlenger, W. E., Fairbank, J. A., Hough, R. L., Jordan, B. K., Marmar, C. R., & Weiss, D. S. **Trauma And The Vietnam Generation: Report Of Findings From The National Vietnam Veterans Readjustment Study**. New York: Brunner/Mazel, (1990b).

Laufer RS, Brett E, Gallops MS. Dimensions of posttraumatic stress disorder among Vietnam veterans. **J Nerv Ment Dis** (1985); 173 (9): 538-545.

Lee, D., & Young, K. Post-Traumatic Stress Disorder: Diagnostic Issues and Epidemiology In Adult Survivors Of Traumatic Events. **International Review Of Psychiatry**, 13, (2001): 150–158.

Livanou, M. Psychological Treatments For Post-Traumatic Stress Disorder: An Overview. **International Review Of Psychiatry,** 13, (2001):181–188.

Luntz BK, Widom CS. Antisocial personality disorder in abused and neglected children grown up. **Am J Psychiatry** (1994);151(5):670-674.

March JS. The nosology of posttraumatic stress disorder. **J Anxiety Disord** (1990); 4: 61-82.

Marmar CR, Weiss DS, Schlenger WE, Fairbank JA, Jordan BK, Kulka RA, Hough RL: Peritrau- Matic Dissociation And Posttraumatic Stress In Male Vietnam Theater Veterans. **American Journal of Psychiatry** 151 (1994):902–907

Marmar CR, Weiss DS, Schlenger WE, Fairbank JA, Jordan BK, Kulka RA, Hough RL. Peritraumatic dissociation and posttraumatic stress in male Vietnam theater veterans. **Am J Psychiatry** (1994); 151(6): 902-907.

Marsella AJ, Friedman MJ, Spain EH,. Ethnocultural Aspects Of Posttraumatic Stress Disorder. **American Psychiatric Press Review Of Psychiatry**, Volume 12. Edited By Oldham, JM, Riba MB, Taskman A, Washington DC, (1993):157–181.

Marsella AJ, Kameoka VA., Ethnocultural Issues In The Assessment Of Psychopathlogy, In Measuring Mental Illness: Psychometric Assessment For Clinicians, S Weltzer (Ed), Washington DC, **American Psychiatric Press**, (1989):229-256.

Mcfarlane AC. The Longitudinal Course Of Posttraumatic Morbidity. The Range Of Outcomes And Their Predictors. **Journal of Nervous and Mental Disase** 176(1), (1988):30-39.

Mcnally R.J. Review Of M. J. Friedman, T. M. Keane, And P. A. Resick 'Handbook Of PTSD: Science And Practice' **Psychological Medicine**, (2008):3-116; 521-540.

Mengüç A., **"Ben Tremeşeli Mehmet Ali"** Comment Grafik Lefkoşa (2013):188-192.

Mengüç A., **"Anılarda Erenköy"** Turk Kultur Kıbrıs, (2005).

Merriam Websters Dictionary: War Http://Www.Merriam-Webster.Com/Dictionary/War Access Date 25.01.2014.

Mollica R.F. Donelan K. Tor S. et. al. The Effect Of Trauma And Confinement On Functional Health And Mental Health Status Of Cambodians Living In Thailand-Cambodia Border Camps. **JAMA** 270 (1993): 581-586.

Mollica R.F. Donelan K. Tor S. Et.al.. The Effect Of Trauma And Confinement On Mollica R.F. Wyshak G. Lavelle J. The Psychosocial Impact Of War Trauma And Torture On Southeast Asian Refugees. **American Journal of Psychiatry** 144 (1987): 1567-1572.

North CS, Smith EM. Spitznagel EL. One-Year Follow-Up Survivors Of A Mass Shooting. **American Journal of Psychiatry** 154 (1997): 1696-1702.

Oberling P., **"The Road To Bellapais: The Turkish Cypriot Exodus To Northern Cyprus"** Social Science Monographs; New York: Distributed by Columbia University Press", (1982).

O'Toole, B. I., Marshall, R. P., Grayson, D. A., et.al. The Australian Vietnam Veterans Health Study: III. Psychological Health Of Australian Vietnam Veterans And Its Relationship To Combat. **International Journal Of Epidemiology**, 25 (1996): 331-339.

Ozer, E. J., Best, S. R., Lipsey, T. L., Weiss, D. S. Predictors Of Posttraumatic Stress Disorder And Symptoms In Adults: A Meta- Analysis. **Psychological Bulletin**, 129 (2003):52–73.

Özgen, F., Aydın H. Travma Sonrası Stres Bozukluğu, **Klinik Psikiyatri** 1, (1999)34-41

Patrick V, Patrick WK. Cyclone'78 In Sri Lanka-The Mental Health Trail. **British Journal of Psychiatry** 138 (1981): 210-216.

Perkonigg, A., Kessler, R. C., Stortz, S., Wittchen, H. U. Traumatic Events And Post-Traumatic Stress Disorder In The Community: Prevalence, Risk Factors And Comorbidity. **Acta Psychiatrica Scandinavica**, 101 (2000) 46–59.

Plumer A.,**"Cyprus, 1963-64 The Fateful Years"** Cyrep Lefkosa (2003).

Pribor EF, Dinwiddie SH. Psychiatric correlates of incest in childhood. **Am J Psychiatry**. 1992; 149(1): 52-56.

Priebe S, Grappasonni I, Mari M, Dewey M, Petrelli F,Costa A. Posttraumatic stress disorder six months after an earthquake: findings from a community sample in a rural region in Italy. **Soc Psychiatry Psychiatr Epidemiol** (2009); 44:393-7.

Ramsey R. Gorst-Unsworth C. Turner S. Psychiatric Morbidity In Survivors Of State Organized Violence Including Torture: A Retrospective Series. **British Journal of Psychiatry** 162 (1993): 55-59.

Resnick HS, Foy DW, Donahoe CP et.al.. Antisocial Behavior And Posttraumatic Stress Disorder In Vietnam Veterans. **Journal of Clinical Psychology**, 45(6) (1989):860-866.

Resnick HS, Kilpatrick DG, Dansky BS et. Al. Prevalence Of Civilian Trauma And PTSD In A Representative National Sample Of Women. **Journal of Consultung Clinical Psychology**, 61(1993): 948-991.

Rosen J, Fields R, Hand A., et al: Concurrent Post-Traumatic Stress Disorder In Psychogeriatric Patients. **The American Journal of Geriatric Psychiatry** 2 (1989): 65-69.

Ruef, A. M., Litz, B. T., Schlenger, W. E. Hispanic ethnicity and risk for combat-related posttraumatic stress disorder. **Cultural Diversity and Ethnic Minority Psychology**, (2000) 6(3), 235-251.

Sadavoyj, Joel et.al. Integrated Psychotherapy For The Elderly. **Canadian Journal of Psychiatry/La Revue canadienne de psychiatrie**, Vol 39(8, Suppl 1), (1994) :19-S26.

Sadrazam H. "Birinci Harekât - Temmuz 1974 (Kıbrıs'ın Savaş Tarihi 3 - Kıbrıs'ta Mitlerden Gerçeğe)" (2013).

Sadrazam H. **"Erenköy Çatışmalarından Yunan Darbesine Kıbrıs'ın Savaş Tarihi 2-Kıbrıs'ta Mitlerden Gerçeğe)"** Cilt 2, (2013).

Sadrazam H. **"Tarihsel Süreçte Kıbrıs'ın Jeopolitik Önemi - Ilk Silah Sesleri - (Kıbrıs'ın Savaş Tarihi 1-Kıbrıs'ta Mitlerden Gerçeğe)"** (2013).

Sağlam, D.,Hocaoğlu,Ç.(2007)Yaşlılarda Travma Sonrası Stres Bozukluğu:Bir Olgu Sunumu.**Klinik Psikiyatri**,10(223-227)

Saigh PA, Bremner JD: The History Of Posttraumatic Stress Disorder, In Posttraumatic Stress Dis- Order: **A Comprehensive Text**. Edited By Saigh PA, Bremner JD. New York, Allyn & Bacon, (1998), Pp 1–17

Sana R, Khattak SUR. Prevalence of post-traumatic stress disorder in flood affected poppulation of Banda Sheikh Ismail, district Nowshera. **J Postgrad Med Inst** (2014); 28(1):27-32.)

Sanver A. **"TMT Ve ÖHD Anılarım"**, (2013).

Sanver A. **"TMT ve ÖHD Anılarım"** Ateş Press Lefkoşa (2012) 80-128

Schlenger, W. E., Kulka, R. A., Fairbank, J. A., Hough, R. L., Jordan, B. K., Marmar, C. R., et al.. The prevalence of post-traumatic stress disorder in the Vietnam generation: A multimethod, multisource assessment of psychiatric disorder. **Journal of Traumatic Stress**, (1992) 5, 333-363.

Schnurr, P. P., Lunney, C. A., & Sengupta, A. Risk factors for the development versus maintenance of posttraumatic stress disorder. **Journal of Traumatic Stress**, (2004) 17, 85-95.

Schnurr, P. P., Lunney, C. A., Sengupta, A., & Waelde, L. C. A descriptive analysis of PTSD chronicity in Vietnam Veterans. **Journal of Traumatic Stress**, (2003) 16, 545-553.

Scott, W.J. **PTSD In DSM-III: A Case In The Politics Of Diagnosis And Disease. Social Problems** (1990) 37(3), 294-310

Shalev AY, Posttraumatic Stress Disorder Among Injured Survivors Of A Terrorist Attack: Predictive Value Of Early Intrusion And Avoidance Symptoms. **Journal of Nervous and Mental Disase** (1992), 180: 505-509

Shore JH, Tatum E, Vollmer WM. Psychiatric Reactions To Disaster: The Mount Saint Helen's Experience. **American Journal of Psychiatry** (1986), 143: 590-595.)

Shore JH, Tatum EL, and Vollmer WM. Evaluation of mental effects of disaster: Mount St. Helen's eruption. **Am J Public Health** (1986); 76(3 Suppl): 76-83.

Silverman AB, Reinherz HZ, Giaconia RM. The long-term sequelae of child and adolescent abuse: a longitudinal community study. **Child Abuse Negl** (1996); 20(8): 709-723.

Sledge, W. H., Boydstun, J. A., & Rabe, A. J. Self-Concept Changes Related To War Captivity. **Archives Of General Psychiatry**, (1980) 37, 430–443.

Solomon SD, Canino GJ. Appropriateness of the DSM-III-R criteria for post-traumatic stress disorder. **Compr Psychiatry** (1990); 31(3): 227-237.

Solomon Z., The Effect Of Combat–Related Posttraumatic Stress Disorder On The Family. **Psychiatry Res** (1988) 51(3):323–329

Solomon Z, Banbenisity R. The Role Of Proximity, Immediacy And Expectancy In Front-Line Treatment Of Combat Stress Reaction Among Israelis In The Lebanon War. **American Journal of Psychiatry** (1986), 143: 613-617

Solomon Z, Miculincer M, Waysman M. Delayed And Immediate Onset Posttraumatic Stress Disorder: I. Differential Clinical Characteristics. **Soc Psychiatriy Psychiatr Epidemiol** (1991), 26(1): 1-7.

Somek E. **"Kıbrıs Türkün Milli Mücadelesi"** Bizim Kitaplar Istanbul (2012), 164-166.

Speed N, Engdahl B, Schwartz J, Eberly R. Posttraumatic stress disorder as a consequence of POW experience. **J Nerv Ment Dis** (1989); 177(3): 147-153.

Speed, N.; Engdahl, B., Schwartz, J. Et.al.. Posttraumatic Stress As A Consequence Of The POW Experience. **Journal of Nervous and Mental Disase** (1989); 177: 147-153

Sümbüloğlu K. Sümbüloğlu V. **"Biyoistatistik"** Hatipoğlu Press Ankara (2007).
Sungur M.Z. Sürmeli B.A. Özçubukçuoğlu A. Common Features Of PTSD Cases Amongst A Group Of Military Staff Referred From The Southeast Region Of Turkey. **J Cognitive Psychotherapy: An International Quarterly** (1995), 9(4): 279-284

Tamçelik, Soyalp "Türk Mukavemet Teşkilatı'nda (TMT) Muhabere Sistemlerinin Özellikleri". **Journal of Cyprus Studies**, C. III, nr. 2 (1997).

Taylak M. **"Saltanat, 2. Meşrutiyet ve 1. Cumhuriyet'te Öğrenci Hareketleri"** Başnur Press Ankara (1969), 257-260.

Thomas M. Leonard. Encyclopedia Of The Developing World, Taylor & Francis,, C. Cockburn. **The Line: Women, Partition, And The Gender Roles In Cyprus**. Volume 1. Zed Books (2006), 96; 429

Turkish Resistance Organisation Source:
http://en.wikipedia.org/wiki/Turkish_Resistance_Organisation?oldid=626309251 access date 10.09.2014

Turner, F., **Echoes Of Combat: Trauma, Memory, And The Vietnam War.** Minneapolis: University Of Minnesota Press. (2001)

United Nations Security Council Resolution 550: "Gravely Concerned About The Further Secessionist Acts In The Occupied Part Of The Republic Of Cyprus Which Are In Violation Of Resolution (1983), 541.

Http://Www.Un.Org/En/Sc/Documents/Resolutions/1984.Shtml Access Date 25.01.2014.

Ursano R.J. Fullerton C.S. Norwood A. Psychiatric Dimensions Of Disaster: Patient Care, Community Consultation And Preventive Medicine. **Harvard Review Of Psychiatry** (1995), 3(4):196-209.

Ursano RJ, Fullerton CS, Kao TC Et. Al. Longitudinal Assessment Of Posttraumatic Stress Disorder And Depression After Exposure To Traumatic Death. **Journal of Nervous and Mental Disase** (1995), 183(1): 36-42.

Volkan V.D. **"Blind Trust/ Large Groups And Their Leaders In Times Of Crisis And Terror"** 3th Edition Okuyan Us Publishing (2012), 79-129.

Volkan V.D. **"Cyprus: War And Adaptation A Psychoanalytic History Of Two Ethnic Groups In Conflict"** Everest Publishing Istanbul (2008) 199-218; 145-169.

Vurana H. **"Kuzey Batı Dillirga"** Mavi Publishing (2011) 560-578; 179-355.

Weine S.M. Vojvoda D. Becker D.F. Et. Al. PTSD Symptoms In Bosnian Refugees One Year After Resettlement In The United States. **American Journal of Psychiatry** (1998), 155: 562-564.

Weine S.M. Vojvoda D. Becker D.F. Et.al. PTSD Symptoms In Bosnaian Refugees One Year After Resettlement In The United States. **American Journal of Psychiatry** (1998), 155: 562-564.

Weiss, D. S., Marmar, C. R., Schlenger, W. E., Fairbank, J. A., Jordan, B. K., Hough, R. L., et al. The prevalence of lifetime and partial post-traumatic stress disorder in Vietnam Theater Veterans. **Journal of Traumatic Stress**, (1992), 5, 365-376.

Wenninger K, Heiman JR. Relating body image to pschological and sexual functioning in child sexual abuse survivors. **J Trauma Stress** (1998); 11(3): 543-562.

World Health Organization. **The ICD-10 classification of mental and behavioural disorders: Clinical descriptions and diagnostic guidelines**. Geneva, Oxford University Press, (1992): 208-210.

Yorgancıoğlu O.M. **"Tutunabilen Son Kök 50. Yılında Erenköy"** Söylem Publishing (2014)

Zimering, R. T., Caddell, J. M., Fairbank, J. A., & Keane, T. M. Post-Traumatic Stress Disorder In Vietnam Veterans: An experimental Validation Of The DSM-III Diagnostic Criteria. **Journal Of Traumatic Stress**, (1993), 6, 327–342.

Zlotnick C, Zakriski AL, Shea MT, Costello E, Begin A, Pearlstein T, Simpson E. The long-term sequelae of sexual abuse: support for a complex posttraumatic stress disorder. **J Trauma Stress** (1996); 9(2): 195-205.

Zlotnick C, Bruce SE, Shea MT, Keller MB, Delayed posttraumatic stress disorder (PTSD) and predictors of first onset of PTSD in patients with anxiety disorders. **J Nerv Ment Dis** (2001) 189(6):404–406.